. . . English style, familiar but not coarse,
elegant but not ostentatious . . .

Samuel Johnson

STYLE

Ten Lessons
in
Clarity
&
Grace

Joseph M. Williams
University of Chicago

Scott, Foresman and Company
Glenview, Illinois

Dallas, Texas   Oakland, New Jersey   Palo Alto, California
Tucker, Georgia   London, England

Excerpt from *Notes of a Native Son* by James Baldwin, copyright
© 1955 by James Baldwin. Reprinted by permission of Beacon Press
and Michael Joseph Ltd.

Excerpt from *Science and the Common Understanding* by J. Robert Oppenheimer,
copyright 1954 by J. Robert Oppenheimer. Reprinted by permission of
Simon & Schuster, a Division of Gulf and Western Corporation.

    2 3 4 5 6   —RRC—   86 85 84 83 82 81

Library of Congress Cataloging in Publication Data

Williams, Joseph M
    Style: ten lessons in clarity and grace.

    Includes index.
    1. English language—Rhetoric. 2. English
language—Style. 3. English language—Business
English. 4. English language—Technical English.
I. Title.
PE1421.W545   808'.042   80-23083
ISBN 0-673-15393-2

To my mother and father

Contents

Preface

To Those Who Write on the Job

Fortunately, most of you require no convincing about the importance of a clear and readable style, especially if you have to waste a large part of your day struggling through the prose of those who have never learned to write well. Unfortunately, the advice that most of us recall about writing well probably doesn't help us correct even our own bad writing. If what we remember is typical of most such advice, it probably consists of banalities such as "Be clear, be concise," or of useless minutiae such as "Don't begin sentences with *and* or end them with prepositions."

The kind of confused writing that most of us have to live with fails for reasons that don't yield to well-meaning but empty generalities, or to any list of particular dos and don'ts. To understand why anyone—including ourselves—writes badly, we have to be able to look at a sentence and understand how it works, how the ideas have been distributed through its different parts, and then decide how to write it better.

To address that problem, we have to be specific and concrete, and that means we have to use some of those terms we may or may not remember from junior high school—*verb, object, noun, active, passive,* and so on. Every subject has a vocabulary which anyone learning that subject has to master. It's the same with style: If you want to understand and improve your own, you have to control a few terms. There aren't a lot of them here, they're not difficult, and every one of them is defined in the Appendix. Under no circumstances waste your time trying to memorize them. Simply learning how to define nouns and verbs won't help you write any better. But if you can develop a sense of how nouns and verbs differ, you'll understand what distinguishes good and bad writing, and *that* will help you write better.

Something I have found repeatedly among those who believe they have a problem with the way people in their organization write is the lack of a common language about writing and its problems. If you are responsible for the writing of others and you find it unacceptable, you have to communicate to those writers more than your displeasure. You have to tell them what to do to write better. Yet time and again I have seen administrators simply ignore the problem because they don't feel confident discussing style: Neither the administrator nor the subordinate has a vocabulary to express what either sees as the source of the difficulty. Or if an administrator does try to explain what's wrong, his or her language will be vague, impressionistic, and probably inconsistent with the language of others in the organization who must also tell their subordinates how to improve their writing.

This book provides the consistent and explicit vocabulary that will let you address a writing problem consistently and explicitly.

To Students

Nothing is more tedious than learning a skill that seems to have no immediate application and no obvious value, even in the distant future. You've already learned how to write well enough to get as far as you've come. And when you read all those textbooks, journal articles, and scholarly monographs written in language so turgid and incomprehensible that it sets one's head to throbbing, the penalty for bad writing must seem to be not especially severe. If someone can write badly and still get published, why should any of us spend the time and effort learning how to write well?

The answer is one that you will have to take partly on faith: First, and most obviously, the very scarcity of clear and precise writing makes it that much more valuable. Even though an unclear and imprecise style obviously does not bar a good many writers from getting into print, a person who can write clearly and gracefully goes out into the world with an uncommon skill. One important reason working business people and professionals do not achieve what their potential might otherwise allow is their inability to communicate, to get their good ideas down on paper in a way that lets others understand those ideas quickly and easily. In every survey that asks business people what subjects they wish they had studied more carefully, their first or second answer is always communication.

True, you might compensate for a turgid style with great ideas, with an original and creative mind. But the more common truth is that most of us have minds and ideas that are closer to merely good than to outstandingly brilliant. And ideas that are only good need all the help they can get. So if we weren't born brilliant, we can at least learn to be clear; it is, in fact, an ability, that is just as rare as inherited genius, and most of the time considerably more useful.

I know how unpersuasive this kind of "let-me-tell-you-what's-good-for-you" argument is when you haven't tested it against hard experience. But in fact, you may already have conducted that test: How often have you wanted to toss aside a textbook or journal article whose every leaden sentence was an agony to read? How many sentences have you reread and reread again, struggling to extract whatever meaning may or may not have sunk under the weight of all that verbiage? How often have you read a dozen pages only to realize that you can't recall a single idea?

You have to read that kind of writing now, perhaps because it's been assigned, perhaps because you need it for a term paper. But suppose for a moment that you were the boss of someone who wrote badly, and that you've just received a memo or report written in that tangled, abstract style. What do you think would be your first impulse?

Finally, the tone of this book is strongly prescriptive. Its lessons will tell you in a straightforward way how to write clearly. I think the advice is sound. I've tested it with a good many adult writers in government, the professions, and business. So far, no one has objected that the problems we will be addressing are irrelevant to the concerns that real writers have in the real world. Quite the contrary: They go to the flabby heart of a terminally opaque style.

But however prescriptive I seem about what counts as clear writing, don't you be reluctant to experiment, to play with different prose styles. Try writing in the ponderous bureaucratic style that this book condemns, simply to get the feel of writing it. Try creating a passage in a style elegant beyond your needs, just to see whether you can pull it off. Try writing the longest sentence you can, just to feel when you've stretched it to its breaking point. Try writing a passage of one curt sentence after another to achieve a sense of breathless haste, or utter certitude.

Language, style, should not be something that boxes you in, but a way to free your intellect and imagination from the obscurity that confused prose puts between you and your ideas.

To Teachers

This book addresses only one major problem of composition: style. It does not take up matters of intention, invention, or organization. Their omission is not an oversight. I intend this to be a short book focusing on the single most serious problem that *mature* writers face: a wordy, tangled, too-complex prose style. For larger matters of form, you will need another book.

I have tried to approach style as process, as an achievement. The first step in that process, of course, is to get something down on paper. But that's the easy part. The serious part of writing is rewriting. Samuel Johnson said it about as well as anyone: "What is written without effort is in general read without pleasure." The effort is more in the editing than in the writing.

I know that many undergraduates have a problem precisely opposite to that which most of this book addresses—a style characterized by one fifteen-word sentence after another. But that's not a problem that seems to endure very long. I have worked with a good many adult writers in government, in the professions, and in business; I have met not one whose major writing problem was a style that was immature. I am encouraged in this observation by every other adult writing program I have ever seen: Not one of them takes up the matter of writing longer rather than shorter sentences.

Now, you might object that there is still no point in addressing a problem that does not yet afflict your students. Two points: First, dealing with this matter now will prepare them to deal with a problem that they all seem destined to develop later. To assume that we should not address a problem before it arises is a little bit like teaching birth control after the rabbit dies.

And second, simply by writing out the new sentences that result from editing those in the exercises, students will come to feel what it is like to write down a sentence longer than ten or fifteen words. Copy and imitation, time-honored ways of teaching writing, will help the less advanced students feel the rhythm and movement that a long but clear sentence demands. After all, if we cannot lead our students through what they are supposed to be learning to do, we ought not be surprised when they do not learn to do it.

The exercises in imitation are directed specifically toward

developing a mature style. Assure your students that they don't have to imitate the model sentences word for word; they have only to imitate the stylistic point being discussed. If they have problems thinking up things to write about, suggest some topics parallel to the subject matter of the model sentences. In fact, you might do the exercises yourself to get a sense of what can and can't be done with them.

All this is intended to anticipate an objection that some readers may raise: The material is appropriate for upper-class students and adults, but it is too difficult for beginning students. I understand why some teachers of freshmen might feel that way. I realize how severely underprepared many first-year students are in matters of both style and grammar. I use a few grammatical terms here. But I confess I am a bit puzzled that any teacher would object to a discussion that introduced terms that a student did not know but should. I have always assumed that we are in the business of teaching students what they do not know, and that if they do not know what *subject, verb, predicate, object,* and so on mean, then we tell them. I don't see how we can avoid using some terminology, even new terminology, any more than a physicist can avoid using new terms such as *lepton, quark,* or *charmed particle* in a textbook on the fundamental structure of matter.

Lesson 9 on style and usage may disconcert more than a few. (Indeed, it already has.) It asserts that some widely circulated "rules" of usage may in fact not be as widely observed by genuinely careful writers as some might think, or wish. Parts of that lesson may read as if I based my observations on some quirky notions of personal usage, privately arrived at. In fact, I have based them on a good deal of reading specifically to find whether those "rules" have any force among otherwise careful writers. I can only assert that in writing which has not been thoroughly edited to make it conform to the "rules" I address, there appear a good many singular *data*s, a good many *which*es for *that*s, a good many prepositions at the ends of sentences, split infinitives, sentences beginning with *and.* Indeed, all these so-called violations of good usage appear in books that have been scrupulously edited.

In the real world of real writers, success depends little on avoiding *contact* as verb or *finalize* meaning more than finish. It depends on the ability to make a point precisely, directly, and persuasively.

"Precision" and "Upholding Standards" have too often meant finding trivial points of usage violated in prose that deserves criticism on far more substantial grounds. Coming down hard on a *which* that we think should be a *that* has for too long been a way of saying, "I don't like what I'm reading very much, but I don't know how else to express my dislike." It is the equivalent of that all-purpose "Awk" that so many among us scribble in the margin when they can't explain what *makes* a sentence awkward.

I hope that what follows will provide a vocabulary that makes the word *precision* more than an expression of imprecise values, and *imprecise* more often an expression of precise displeasure.

To All

Devoured in one piece, this book will surely seem indigestible. It does not have the leisurely pace of an occasional essay that can be read in one or two sittings. The lessons are compact: read quickly, they will seem dense, even overwhelming. Take them in small chunks. Do a section at a time, up to the exercises. Do the exercises; find someone else's writing to edit; find some old writing of your own and edit it. Then look hard at what you've written today—first only for the point of the lesson, or section. Then go through it a second time, looking for another point, and if you have the time, again for other points. If you try to edit everything at once, a sentence will dissolve into a confusion of words.

I have organized the lessons as if I were editing my own prose. In Lesson 2, I concentrate on getting the backbone of a sentence straight, on getting the crucial ideas in the right grammatical places with the right grammatical connections. In Lesson 3, I address the problem of clearing away that wordy underbrush that can choke off the flow of your ideas. In Lesson 4, I take up the problem of excessively long sentences: Even when you've expressed your ideas cleanly and clearly, you can still pack too many of them into a single sentence. In Lesson 5, I discuss how to make a long sentence clear and fluent, how to avoid the discontinuities and interruptions that can confuse your reader.

Once I've edited my individual sentences so that I can understand what, if anything, I have to say, then I can get a better idea whether the whole thing hangs together, whether it is a cohesive and coherent whole, or whether all that verbiage obscured even from me the fact that I hadn't thought through my ideas. Lesson 6 concentrates on making your sentences hang together.

Lesson 7 reviews lessons 2–6 from the point of view of those who have some special reason to write in a way that is maximally clear for minimally prepared readers. Lesson 8 addresses the matter of grace notes, of writing a prose that is more than merely utilitarian. And in Lessons 9 and 10, I take up those issues that we attend to in our final editing: questions of usage and punctuation. In both lessons, I also suggest how to use these small matters to achieve a style a cut above the usual.

So many have provided useful criticism and welcome support that I cannot possibly thank them all. But I must begin with my English 194 students who put up with so many badly typed and faintly dittoed pages, and a teacher who was at times as puzzled over matters of style as they. Their interrest in clear and concise writing compensated for a lot of tedious hours editing their papers. They have been a pleasure to teach, and their subsequent comments about the importance of what they have learned have been gratifying. I thank you all.

I have considerable intellectual debts to those who have broken ground in psycholinguistics, text linguistics, discourse analysis, functional sentence perspective, and so on. Those of you who keep up with such matters will recognize the influence of Charles Fillmore, Jan Firbas, Nils Enkvist, Michael Halliday, Noam Chomsky, Thomas Bever, Vic Yngve, and others. I know I have been influenced more than a little by Robert Graves and Alan Hodge, H. B. Fowler, H. L. Mencken, and surely by E. B. White. I would like to think that I have made explicit what Mr. White advises and has done for so long. Maine air must be, I think, a powerful astringent to style.

I am very grateful to colleagues who have taken time from their own busy lives to read the work of another. At such times, the word *community* in Community of Scholars takes on a special meaning. Whatever quality this book may have is due in large part to their care, time, and energy. I must thank in particular Randy Berlin, Ken Bruffee, Douglas Butturff, Donald Byker, Bruce Campbell, Elaine Chaika, Avon Crismore, Don Freeman, Constance Gefvert, Maxine Hairston, George Hoffman, Ted Lowe, Susan Miller, Neil

Nakadate, Mike Pownall, Peter Priest, Margaret Shaklee, Nancy Sommers, Mary Taylor, and Stephen Witte.

I would also like to acknowledge the assistance of Frederick C. Mish, editorial director, G. & C. Merriam Company, in locating the best examples of three citations in Lesson 9.

The editors at Scott, Foresman saved me from more than a few stylistic gaffes: Shirley Stone and especially Dave Ebbitt, whose editing pen has a very sharp point.

I would like to thank most profoundly the editor who first urged me to write this book, Harriett Prentiss. I am most grateful to her.

And finally, to my family—my thanks for your love and support and understanding, especially when Daddy's "just one minute" stretched to an hour or two.

J. M. W.
Manset, Maine

Lesson One

Toward Clarity

If thought corrupts language, language can also corrupt thought.

George Orwell

Everything that can be thought at all can be thought clearly.
Everything that can be said can be said clearly.

Ludwig Wittgenstein

With precious few exceptions, all the books on style in English are by writers
quite unable to write.

H. L. Mencken

This is a short book based on a simple thesis: It's good to write clearly, and anyone can.

No one would argue with the first part of that claim, least of all those who regularly have to translate prose like this:

> There is now no effective mechanism for introducing into the initiation and development stages of reporting requirements information on existing reporting and guidance on how to minimize burden associations with new requirements.

But the second part of the claim might be disputed by a good many who labor at writing more clearly than that but still end up with prose that hides their ideas not just from their readers but sometimes even from themselves.

Now, we can write prose that fails for reasons more important than an unclear style. If we're as confused about our point when we finish a job of writing as when we began, our writing will be confused too. If we ignore what our readers have to know if they're to understand our ideas, then what we write will surely bewilder them. And if we can't find a way to organize our ideas clearly for our specific audience, then what we write will almost certainly lack that sense of direction and purpose that all coherent prose demands.

As important as those problems are, though, this book specifically addresses a different matter: Once we've learned how to write sentences that are grammatically correct and acceptably punctuated, once we've learned how to focus our ideas, how to gather and organize the information we need to move a clearly defined audience to a specific end, we still have to get those ideas down on paper in a form that is not just grammatically correct but clear and concise enough to be effective.

That is the aim of this book: to explain how you can overcome the one problem that has afflicted generations of mature writers—the problem of an inflated tangle of words, an unnecessarily complex prose style. When we find this kind of writing in government regulations and directives, we call it *bureaucratese;* when we find it in legal contracts and judicial pronouncements, we call it *legalese;* when we find it in scholarly articles and books that inflate simple ideas into gassy and empty abstractions, we call it *academese.* Partly because we find it almost everywhere we look, some believe that it must be the style of institutional success. It is more often the style of academic pretension or bureaucratic intimidation. Wherever we find it, it is a style that, once we see through it, must finally infuriate us.

But anyone familiar with English prose has to wonder whether we can do anything that will substantially improve it. In the early sixteenth century, when English first became respectable enough to replace French and Latin as England's institutional language, our first impulse toward elegance resulted in a style thick with Latinate abstraction, a weakness to which English writers have surrendered ever since.

By the middle of the seventeeth century, an inflated style had infected the sciences. Shortly after the Royal Society was established in 1660, one of its historians complained,

> . . . of all the studies of men, nothing may sooner be obtained
> than this vicious abundance of phrase, this trick of metaphors, this
> volubility of tongue which makes so great a noise in the
> world . . . .
> —Thomas Sprat, *History of the Royal Society,* 1667

When the New World was settled, we had a chance to create a new prose style lean and sinewy enough to suit a people civilizing a continent. But American writers have no more escaped chronic bloat and abstraction than have the English. James Fenimore Cooper asserted, not too simply and directly himself, that "the common faults of American language are an ambition of effect, a want of simplicity, and a turgid abuse of terms." Henry David Thoreau agreed: "All men are really attracted by the beauty of plain speech [but they] write in a florid style in imitation of this."

We read the same sentiments today. On the language of the social sciences:

> . . . a turgid and polysyllabic prose does seem to prevail in the
> social sciences . . . . Such a lack of ready intelligibility, I believe,
> usually has little or nothing to do with the complexity of thought.
> It has to do almost entirely with certain confusions of the
> academic writer about his own status.
> —C. Wright Mills, *The Sociological Imagination*

On the language of medicine:

> It now appears that obligatory obfuscation is a firm tradition within the medical profession . . . . [Medical writing] is a highly skilled, calculated attempt to confuse the reader . . . . A doctor feels he might get passed over for an assistant professorship because he wrote his papers too clearly—because he made his ideas seem too simple.
>
> —Michael Crichton, *New England Journal of Medicine*

And on the language of law:

> . . . in law journals, in speeches, in classrooms and in courtrooms, lawyers and judges are beginning to worry about how often they have been misunderstood, and they are discovering that sometimes they cannot even understand each other.
>
> —Tom Goldstein, *New York Times*

(The abuse heaped on government prose is too familiar to need special testimony here.)

Most adults, I suspect, write in the ways referred to for some combination of just two or three reasons. The first is one just cited: We use complicated language to hide not only simple ideas but even their absence. Impenetrable prose will impress those who confuse difficulty with substance—and there are many who do. Why else so much of it?

In the same way, we use difficult and therefore intimidating language to protect what we have from those who want a share of it: the power, prestige, and privilege that go with being part of the ruling class. We can keep knowledge from those who would use it by locking it up, but we can also hide ideas behind language so impenetrable that only those trained in its use can find them.

Another reason some of us write badly is that we are seized by the memory of an English teacher for whom the only kind of good writing was writing free of errors which only that teacher could understand: fused genitives, dangling participles, split infinitives, and other exotic *disjecta membra*. For many such writers, a blank page is now a minefield that they gingerly traverse, preoccupied less with clarity and precision than with sheer survival.

But the most common reason for bad writing is, I think, the simplest: Most writers just never learn how to write clearly and directly in the first place. No one has ever told them how to edit syntactic confusion into clear prose. Or even that they should try. I say this because I have never met anyone who was anything but delighted to learn and to use the few simple rules that are needed to edit an unreadable tangle into clear, straightforward prose.

Now, in fact, when we address the matter of clear prose, we indirectly address some of those more general problems that I referred to before—problems of organization, intention, and audience. The very act of writing and rewriting helps us clarify our ideas, better understand what we want to say, find the best way to organize our material, and speak to the real interests and needs of our readers. If we can't see through our own confused style to the substance of our ideas, we won't be able to understand ourselves well enough to use the very act of writing to sharpen our ideas, our intentions, and our organization. When we write page after page of impenetrable prose, we finally lose track of our own train of thought: The mere effort to penetrate every sentence finally distracts us from the substance of our ideas.

Writing can be a fruitfully circular process: We have to understand what we want to say in order to write it clearly and concisely. But if we can't write what we mean clearly and concisely enough or, when necessary, clearly and complexly, we won't be able to understand exactly what we are—or could be—saying. If we can write and then quickly rewrite syntactic confusion into clear prose, we'll understand our ideas better. And when we understand our ideas better, we'll write more clearly, and if we write more clearly, we'll understand even better . . . and so it goes, until we run out of energy, interest, or time.

For some of us, that moment may come months or years after we begin. But for most of us, it's closer to tomorrow morning. Few of us enjoy the luxury of ruminating for weeks and months over our prose, writing and rewriting to work out our ideas in a leisurely and reflective sort of way, polishing every phrase and clause to a lapidary finish. Most of us have to be satisfied with a less polished but still useful product.

But that only makes a clear, direct style more important: If we don't have the time to ponder over every sentence as we write, we have to be able to get our ideas down quickly and surely the first time, and then to edit our first draft into something clear, simple, and direct.

But as important as directness and clarity may be, there are times when we want to go beyond it, to a style that is a bit more self-consciously crafted, to a style that may even be just a bit elegant:

> Now the trumpet summons us again—not as a call to bear arms, though arms we need; not as a call to battle, though embattled we are; but a call to bear the burden of a long twilight struggle, year in and year out, "rejoicing in hope, patient in tribulation," a struggle against the common enemies of man: tyranny, poverty, disease and war itself.
>
> —John F. Kennedy, Inaugural Address, January 20, 1961

Not all of us are called upon to write a presidential inaugural address, but sometimes our intentions require that we invest even our most modest prose with more than simple clarity. The last few lessons speak to that matter.

About fifty years ago, H. L. Mencken wrote,

> With precious few exceptions, all the books on style in English are by writers quite unable to write. The subject, indeed, seems to exercise a special and dreadful fascination over school ma'ams, bucolic college professors, and other such pseudoliterates . . . . Their central aim, of course, is to reduce the whole thing to a series of simple rules—the overmastering passion of their melancholy order, at all times and everywhere.

This melancholy judgment has hovered over every sentence I've written here. And Mencken is right: No one can teach a clear style by rule, simple or not, especially to those who have nothing to say and no reason to say it, to those who cannot think or feel or see.

But I know that there are many who do think carefully and feel deeply and see clearly but who still cannot write well. I also know that learning to write well can help us think and feel and see, and that in fact there are some simple and straightforward rules that help.

Here they are.

Lesson Two

The

Grammar of Clarity

Suit the action to the word, the word to the action.

William Shakespeare, *Hamlet*, 3.2

Action is eloquence.

William Shakespeare, *Coriolanus*, 3.2

We don't lack words to praise good writing: clear, direct, readable, precise, and so on. But words like these reflect only how we *feel* about writing; they don't tell us what good writing *is*. We need a way to talk about writing that tells us what is there on the page that makes us feel as we do. Some measures of good writing, for example, simply ask us to count the number of syllables and words and clauses* (the fewer the better, according to some).[1]

But if for every sentence* we wrote, we had to count all the syllables and words and clauses, we'd spend more time counting than writing. And even if counting did tell us which sentences were more or less easy to read, we wouldn't need to count if we learned simply to sense on our own when a passage was clear and direct, or tangled and obscure.

We don't have to count syllables and words in these two sentences to recognize which is clear and which isn't:

> Our lack of pertinent data prevented determination of committee action effectiveness in fund targeting to areas of greatest assistance need.

> Because we lacked pertinent data, we could not determine whether the committee had targeted funds to areas that needed assistance the most.

The real difference between those two sentences isn't in the number of words or syllables or clauses, but in how a writer organizes what he wants to say, how he uses subjects* and verbs* to express who is—or is not—doing what to whom. If we are going to understand why that second sentence is more precise, more direct, we have to understand how the nouns* and verbs, subjects and objects* of those two sentences support the ideas they express.

GRAMMAR AND MEANING

We can state the first principle of clear writing easily enough: Try to state who's doing what in the subject of your sentence, and try to state what that who is doing in your verb. In the second sentence, the writer names in the subject of each clause who acts or who is

---

[1]Throughout this book, terms marked with an asterisk* are defined in the Appendix.

responsible for each action*, and expresses in specific verbs what those actors do:

Subject		Verb
we	⟶	lacked
we	⟶	could not determine
the committee	⟶	targeted
areas	⟶	needed

In the first sentence, on the other hand, the writer says who is doing what to whom much less directly and explicitly. He expresses actions not in verbs but in abstract nouns: *lack, determination, action, assistance, need.* And the writer identifies the agents, the doers of those actions, not in subjects but in prepositional phrases* or in modifiers tacked onto nouns:

our lack . . . committee action effectiveness . . . areas

Or the agent of the action doesn't appear in the sentence at all. In that first sentence, for example, how do we know who makes the determination?

Our lack of pertinent data prevented (whose?) determination . . . .

In short, the clearer and more direct sentence uses its subjects and verbs and objects—the major sentence parts—to state its meaning directly. The first does not.

There are other principles of good writing, and in following lessons, we'll get to them. But this first principle—expressing actions in verbs, and putting the agents of those actions into subjects—goes to the heart of a clear style. Get that straight, and the rest of the sentence begins to fall into place.

VERBS AND ACTIONS

A clear and direct style depends first on how we express action. As we'll use the word here, action will cover many notions: movement, feeling, process, change, activity, condition—physical or mental, literal or figurative. The important point is this: While we cannot always express action in a verb, in the clearest and most vigorous sentences, we usually do. Compare the verbs in these pairs of sentences:

> There will *be* a suspension of these programs by the dean until his reevaluation of their progress *has occurred.*

> The dean *will suspend* these programs until he *reevaluates* their progress.

> At the time of several congressional committee investigations of the CIA, they *performed* no intelligence collection analysis.

> Several congressional committees *investigated* the CIA, but they *did not analyze* how the CIA *collected* intelligence data.

Suspend and *reevaluate* are more specific than *be* and *occur.* *Investigated, collected,* and *analyzed* are more specific than *performed.*

In the next four sentences, the meaning becomes increasingly clear as the action expressed by their verbs becomes increasingly specific:

> There *has been* the exercise of effective staff information dissemination control on the part of the secretary.

> The secretary *has exercised* effective staff information dissemination control.

> The secretary *has* effectively *controlled* staff information dissemination.

> The secretary *has* effectively *controlled* the way the staff *disseminates* information.

The crucial actions here aren't *be* or *exercise* but *control* and *disseminate.*

When we regularly express an important action not as a verb but as a noun, our prose will read like that confused and sluggish writing so common in government, business, and the professions. In chronically indirect and tangled prose, the writer does not express the action of paying by the verb *pay* but by the noun *payment* (or the verbose *compensation*); the action of studying not by the verb *study,* but by the noun *study* (or the more weighty *in-depth investigation*); the action of needing not by the verbs *need* or *must* but as the noun *need* (or the more turgid *urgent requirement*). And then the writer clumps those nouns together into one long compound* noun phrase. As a consequence, we may have to wade through,

> There is a student loan repayment reliability study need.

or worse,

> There is an urgent requirement for a student loan recompensation reliability in-depth investigation.

instead of skimming through,

> We must find out how reliably students repay their loans.

Most writers of pompous prose use their verbs not to express specific actions but merely to state that those actions exist:

We *conducted* an **investigation** of it.	= We *investigated* it.
A **need** *exists* for greater candidate **selection efficiency.**	= We *must select* candidates more *efficiently*.
There *is* the **possibility** of prior **approval** of it.	= He *may approve* of it ahead of time.
A **review** *was done* of the relevant regulations.	= They *reviewed* the relevant regulations.
We *had* a **discussion** of the matter.	= We *discussed* the matter.
The establishment of a different **approach** on the part of the committee *has become* a **necessity.**	= The committee *has to* *approach* it differently.

When your prose seems out of focus, fuzzy and imprecise, look for the important action, the central process or condition. If it typically appears in a noun, set off somewhere between empty verbs and prepositions, your style surely suffers from that bloat and abstraction that makes so much institutional prose thoroughly unreadable. Recast the sentence. Put the crucial action in the verb. And if an important condition or quality is expressed in a noun instead of an adjective* or adverb*, get rid of the noun and use the adjective or adverb:

> There was *precision* in the *preparation* of the data.

> They *prepared* the data *precisely*.

> She exhibited considerable *intelligence* in regard to that.

> She was *intelligent* about that.

Because we use this kind of noun derived from a verb or adjective so often, it would be useful if we had a term for it. We'll call it a *nominalization**, a word that is itself a noun made out of a verb, *nominalize*. Here are some examples:

Verb	Nominalization	Adjective	Nominalization
discover	discovery	careless	carelessness
move	movement	difficult	difficulty
resist	resistance	different	difference
react	reaction	elegant	elegance
hope	hope	equal	equality

Nominalization sounds like jargon, but it's useful. It expresses in a single word what most afflicts a sentence such as,

> There is a *need* for *reanalysis* of our data.

or worse,

> There is a data *reanalysis need*.

instead of,

> We *must reanalyze* our data.

SUBJECTS AND AGENTS

Just as a verb and an action naturally go together, so do subject and agent*. An agent is the source, the initiator, the party or thing ultimately responsible for the action or condition that a sentence refers to. And we can immediately recognize what happens to a style when we put that agent some place other than the subject (usually because we've nominalized our important verbs):

> Determination of foreign policy takes place at the *presidential* level.
>
> *The President* determines foreign policy.
>
> A need for a reevaluation of his condition by *a doctor* exists.
>
> *A doctor* should reevaluate his condition.

Notice that in each case, the second sentence is more direct because the agent appears in the subject and the important action appears in the verb.

In many cases, we omit the agent altogether—most often in a passive* sentence. Compare the passive (which here omits the agent) and the more explicit active* (which states the agent in the subject):

> Passive: Who should be admitted to nuclear energy facilities has not yet been determined.
>
> Active: *The Nuclear Regulatory Commission* has not yet determined whom *it* should admit to nuclear energy facilities.

Nominalizations also let us drop out the agent:

> A need for a reevaluation of his condition exists.
>
> The discovery in regard to the identification and classification of mutant genes has been acknowledged.
>
> There is as yet an absence of nuclear energy facility access determination.

We can have different kinds of agents, including collective agents:

> *Faculties* that achieve national eminence do not always do the best teaching.

secondary or remote agents:

> *Mayor Daley* built Chicago into a giant among cities.

and even seeming agents that figuratively stand for a real agent:

> *The White House* announced today the end of price controls.
>
> *The business sector* refuses to cooperate in the establishment of guidelines.
>
> *Most instances of malignant tumors* fail to seek prompt medical attention.

In some sentences, we use subjects to name things that are really the means, the instrument, by which some unstated agent performs its action.

> *Studies* of coal production reveal these figures.
>
> *These new data* establish the need for more detailed analysis.
>
> *This evidence* proves my theory.

That is,

> When *we study* coal production, we find these figures.
>
> *I have established* through these new data that we must analyze the problem in more detail.
>
> With this evidence *I can prove* my theory.

Regardless of the precise sense of agency we express in a subject, whether it's literal or figurative, a real agency or its instrument, the first principle of a clear and direct style remains the same:

> As often as you can, use verbs to express the central action and use the subject to express a strong sense of its agency.

Now we have to understand that this is only a useful guide, not an exceptionless rule. We will be looking at sentences later where to be clear, we have to violate this principle. But if you *consistently* express action in abstract nouns and *consistently* use verbs such as *do, make, have, be, perform, occur,* verbs that are almost meaningless because they are so general, then you are probably writing prose that is both graceless and unclear. There is no golden mean to aim at here, no ideal proportion of nominalizations (though more than one in every six or seven words will almost always prove to be too many). The real point is to develop a sense of when your prose moves with the clarity and vigor that only precise subjects and strong verbs provide. And to know how to correct your prose when it doesn't.

OBJECTS AND GOALS

As agent is to subject and action is to verb, so goal* is to object:

subject	verb	object
agent	action	goal

A goal is that toward which an agent directs its action or attention. It's whatever is changed, affected, created, attended to, influenced, transformed, moved, as a result of some other force.

One of the traditional definitions of a direct object* is a noun that follows a transitive* verb:

> We described *the scene.*

> Japan has exported *large amounts of steel.*

> Local politics reflects *grass roots sentiments.*

We ordinarily express a goal as a direct object:

> Shakespeare wrote *Hamlet.*

But there are exceptions: The subject of a passive verb is typically a goal:

> *Hamlet* was written by Shakespeare.

The goal can also be the subject of a small number of active* verbs:

> *His ideas* received my constant criticism.

The personnel experienced a sharp cutback.

Our recommendations went through several reviews.

While it's useful to be able to identify objects and goals, the more important parts of a sentence are its subject and agent, its verb and action. When subjects and verbs clearly express agents and their actions, the objects and goals will usually take care of themselves.

SOME FINE POINTS: Revising Nominalizations

A few common patterns of abstract nominalizations are easy to spot and revise.

1. When the nominalization is the subject of an empty verb, change the nominalization to a verb and find a new subject:

   Our *intention* **is** to audit the records of the program.

   We *intend* to audit the records of the program.

   Our *discussion* **concerned** a tax cut.

   We *discussed* a tax cut.

2. When the nominalization follows an empty verb, change the nominalization to a verb that replaces the empty verb.

   The police **conducted** an *investigation* into the matter.

   The police *investigated* the matter.

   The committee **has** no *expectation* that it will meet the deadline.

   The committee does not *expect* to meet the deadline.

3. When the nominalization follows a *there is* or *there are,* change the nominalization to a verb that replaces the *is* or *are* and find a subject:

   There is a *need* for further *study* of this program.

   The engineering staff *must study* this program further.

   There was considerable *erosion* of the land from the floods.

   The floods considerably *eroded* the land.

4. When a nominalization in a subject is linked to another
nominalization in the predicate* by a verb or a phrase that
expresses some kind of logical connection such as cause and
effect, condition and consequence, revise as follows: (a)
change both abstractions to verbs, (b) find the subject of
those verbs, and (c) link the new clauses with a word that
expresses the logical connection.

To express cause: *because, since, when*

To express condition: *if, provided that*

To express reservation: *though, although*

Schematically, we do this:

The group's failure [was the result of] its chairman's resignation.
modifier noun | modifier noun
subject verb | subject verb
The group failed because its chairman resigned.

Data *analysis* must be done immediately subsequent to its *collection*.

The data must be *analyzed* immediately *after* it is *collected*.

And we could make this active, with agents in the subject position:

You must analyze the data immediately after *you collect* it.

Some further examples:

The *discovery* of a method for the *manufacture* of artificial skin will
have the result of a great increase in the *survival* of patients with
radical burns.

—Researchers *discover* a way to *manufacture* artificial skin . . . .
—More patients *will survive* radical burns . . . .

If researchers can discover a way to manufacture artificial skin,
many more patients will survive radical burns.

The presence of extensive rust *damage* to the exterior surfaces
prevented immediate *repairs* to the hull.

—Rust had extensively *damaged* the exterior surfaces . . . .
—We could not *repair* the hull immediately . . . .

Because rust had extensively damaged the exterior surfaces, we could not repair the hull immediately.

The *instability* of the motor housing did not preclude the *completion* of the field trials.

—The motor housing was *unstable* . . . .
—The research staff *completed* field trials . . . .

Even though the motor housing was unstable, the research staff completed the field trials.

5. When you have two nominalizations in a row, turn at least the first into a verb. Then either leave the second as it is or turn it into a verb in a clause beginning with *how* or *why:*

There was first a *review* of the *evolution* of the medial dorsal fin.

First, she *reviewed* the *evolution* of the medial dorsal fin.

First, she *reviewed how* the medial dorsal fin *evolved.*

The President could offer no *explanation* for his *popularity decline.*

The President could not *explain* his *popularity decline.*

The President could not *explain* why his popularity had *declined* (or *the decline in his popularity*).

USEFUL NOMINALIZATIONS

In some cases, nominalizations are useful, even necessary. Don't bother changing these:

1. The nominalizaton is a subject referring to an idea in a previous sentence:

These arguments all depend on a single unproven claim.

This decision can lead to costly consequences.

Such an agreement is in everyone's best interests.

This lets us link sentences into a more cohesive flow.

2. The nominalization names what would be the object of its verb:

I do not understand either *her meaning* or *his intention.*

rather than the wordier:

> I do not understand either *what she means* or *what he intends.*

We don't improve these much by changing nominalizations into clauses.

3. In place of *the fact that,* a nominalization will usually save a few words:

> *The fact that I denied* what he accused me of impressed the jury.

> *My denial* of his accusations impressed the jury.

(In that sentence, a nominalization *accusation* also replaced the *what*-clause.)

4. The nominalization is a term so commonly used that it has virtually lost its value as a significant action:

> Few issues have so deeply divided American politics as *abortion* on *demand.*

> The Equal Rights *Amendment* will certainly become an issue in this year's *election.*

> *Taxation* without *representation* was not the central concern of the American *Revolution.*

In each of those sentences, the abstract nominalization refers to a fixed idea that we refer to over and over again. Rather than spell out that idea every time in a full-blown clause, we contract it into a single noun, or compound noun. In this case, the nominalization is more economical and direct than the full clause.

And of course, some nominalizations name abstract ideas that we can express only in a nominalization: *freedom, death, love, despair, hope, life, wisdom.* If we couldn't turn some verbs or adjectives into nouns, we would find it difficult—perhaps impossible—to discuss subjects that have preoccupied us for millennia. You simply have to develop an eye for when the nominalization expresses one of these ideas and when it hides a significant action:

> There has been a *demand* for an end to *taxation* on entertainment.

> We *demand* that the government not *tax* entertainment.

Exercise 2-I

Rewrite these into a more direct style. In 1–5, both agents and actions are in italics. State the agents as subjects and the actions as verbs.

1. *Our expectation* was to establish new tolerance levels.
2. *Attempts* were made on the part of the *engineering staff* in regard to an *assessment* of the project.
3. There were *expectations* by the *governing committee* that *their* report *submission* would meet the deadline.
4. The *appearance* of the *candidate* before the board was on June 30.
5. *The governor's refusal* of the request is a *necessity*.

In 6–10, only agents are in italics.

6. A *presidential* appeal was made to *the American people* for the conservation of gasoline.
7. More accurate measurements of the thorium half-life were conducted at that time by *independent investigators*.
8. Discussions by the *participants* of the future of the program were conducted amicably.
9. There was no independent *business-sector* analysis of the cause of the trade deficit.
10. Agreement as to the need for revisions in the terms of the treaty was reached by *the two sides*.

In 11–15, only the actions are in italics.

11. There was *uneasiness* among management over the result of the survey.
12. There must be thorough *preparation* of the specimen sections by the laboratory personnel.
13. The discrepancy in the data demands *checking* by the insurer.
14. The *rejection* of the application by the dean was unexpected.
15. The performance by the police of an *investigation* into the affair occurred without delay.

In the next eleven items, neither agent nor action is identified. Where no agent is expressed, invent one.

16. There should be no hesitation in regard to saying no.
17. The same principles of bilateral symmetry received study after the last report.
18. A solution to the problem of UFOs will never be found by the Air Force.
19. It is my belief that there should be consultation by the administrators with the student body before changes in rules are made.
20. Cutbacks in loan availability are mandated as a result of lack of success in the acquisition of federal funding.
21. A redetermination of their personnel needs is necessary before assistance from local sources can be provided.
22. Complete replacement of corneal tissue depends on the successful suppression of immunoresponse mechanisms.
23. It would be an oversimplification of the problem for me to put forth the argument that all government officials exhibit inefficient and wasteful administrative behavior.
24. A significant contribution to the literature on the subject is Goywzc's specification of the causes for emigration from environments with a lack of sufficient capital base.
25. While methods for the corroboration of reliability and validity of respondents' responses have been under development by social scientists, there were none employed in the present study, making reliance on respondents' exaggerated estimates of their situation fraught with unreliability.
26. The reason of greatest importance for the writing of a prose of maximal clarity and directness possible is the following. The grinding out of a sentence that is choked with noun abstractions and passive limpness and that seems to be syntactically labyrinthian rather than an attempt at speaking with directness to an audience's mind has the possibility of being a deception of yourself as well as your audience. The writing of a sentence with one Latinate noun rumbling after another can lead to the belief that something of importance has been said, regardless of the actuality of it. The editing away of the rumble has the result of the discovery that what is thought to be thundering prose is an empty barrel's echo, in reality.

NOUN + NOUN + NOUN

Another habit of style that will keep you from linking one idea to another clearly and explicitly is the long compound noun phrase. This habit is especially common among scholarly and technical writers:

> *Early childhood thought disorder misdiagnosis* often occurs as a result of unfamiliarity with recent *research literature* describing such conditions. This paper is a review of seven recent studies in which are findings of particular relevance to *preteen hyperactivity diagnosis* and to *treatment modalities* involving *medication maintenance level evaluation procedures.*

Many grammarians insist that we should never modify one noun with another, but such a rule would keep us from using such common phrases as *stone wall, student committee,* and *radio telescope.* We can more persuasively reject such phrases on the grounds that most of them are awkward or, worse, ambiguous, especially when they include one or more nominalizations. They may be more economical than the fully articulated phrase, and they may be entirely acceptable in scientific and technical writing. But they are graceless all the same. And when we recognize their potential ambiguity, we may decide that in the long run the very slight economy in words is a bad bargain.

Whenever you find in your writing a string of consecutive nouns, try unpacking the phrase. Start from the last noun and reverse their order, rewriting the string into explicit prepositional phrases. If one of the nouns is a nominalization, rewrite it into a full verb. For example, here is the first compound noun phrase in the sample paragraph:

early childhood thought disorder misdiagnosis
1   2   3   4

misdiagnosis   disorder   thought   childhood
4   3   2   1

(At this point we can see where the ambiguity lies: What's early, the childhood, the disorder, or the diagnosis? We'll set the problem aside for the moment.) Now rewrite the string into a full phrase, using a verb if you can:

misdiagnose disordered thought in childhood

If we unpack the other phrases and reassemble them into a complete sentence, we get something a bit clearer:

> Physicians are misdiagnosing disordered thought in young children because they are unfamiliar with the literature on recent research.

You can lighten the rhythm of a sentence if you also watch for possessive nouns, nouns that have an apostrophe in them:

> *The city's sales tax position* toward an increase contradicts *the State Finance Office's recent announcement.*

You can translate most possessive nouns into prepositional phrases:

> The position *of* the city toward a sales tax increase contradicts a recent announcement *from* the State Finance Office.

Don't apply this advice to human or animal possessive nouns. For some reason, they seem less heavy than nonhuman possessive nouns:

> The *President's intention* to reach an agreement with the Soviet Union on Afghanistan depends on Senator *Jackson's support.*

Exercise 2-II

Turn the compound noun phrases in 1–5 into prepositional phrases.

1. The plant safety standards committee discussed recent air quality regulation announcements.
2. Diabetic patient blood pressure reduction may be a consequence of renal extract depressor agent application.
3. Pancreatic gland motor phenomena are regulated chiefly by parasympathetic nervous system cells.
4. The main goal of this article is to describe text comprehension processes and recall protocol production.
5. On the basis of these principles, we may now attempt to formulate narrative information extraction rules.

In these next sentences, unpack compound nouns and edit the indirect style by placing agents and actions in subjects and verbs. Invent agents where necessary.

6. This paper is an investigation into information processing behavior involved in computer human cognition simulation games.
7. Enforcement of guidelines for new car model tire durability is a Federal Trade Commission responsibility.
8. Upon court appearance by the defendant, courtroom legal service will be effected by the presiding justice with the request for time requirement waiver so that the case hearing can begin.
9. The Social Security program is a standard monthly income floor guarantee for individuals whose benefit package potential is based on a determination of lifelong contribution schedule.
10. Based on extensive training needs assessment reviews and on selected CETA office site visits, there was the identification of concepts and issues to constitute an initial staff questionnaire instrument.
11. Corporation organization under state law supervision has resulted in federal government inability as to effective implementation of pollution reduction measures.
12. Determination of support appropriateness for community organization assistance need was precluded by difficulty in the obtaining of data relevant to a committee activity review.
13. The secretary of the Department of Energy's November 1, 1979, press release announcement was to the effect that there was a decision for surplus alcohol stock disposal on the part of major manufacturers as a result of the October 28 meeting discussions between the manufacturers and the DOE.
14. The existence of these aforementioned conditions in regard to improper reimbursement claims is due to compliance failure of relevant school personnel with food-service reimbursement claim policies and to student reimbursement claim reviews being ineffective or inadequate.
15. The art of cardiac sound interpretation requires an

intimate cardiac physiology and cardiac disease pathophysiology knowledge.

PASSIVES

In addition to avoiding abstract nominalizations and long compound noun phrases, you can make your style more vigorous and direct if you also avoid unnecessary passive verbs. Now there are many occasions when you should choose the passive; we'll look at some of those occasions in a moment. But when you use passives to excess, when almost every verb is passive, your style will slow to a crawl. And when you combine passives with nominalizations and compound noun phrases, you will create that wretched prose we call medicalese, sociologese, educationese, bureaucratese: all of the *-eses* of those who confuse authority and objectivity with polysyllabic abstraction and remote impersonality.

In passive sentences, the subject expresses the goal of an action; a form of *be* always precedes a past participle* form of the verb; and the agent may or may not be expressed in a *by*-phrase:

> Active: The partners   broke   the agreement.
>
> Passive: The agreement   was broken   by the partners.

Passive order reverses the more direct order of agent-action-goal; it is an order that will eventually cripple the sense of easy movement that characterizes an energetic style.

Compare these passages:

> It *was found* that information concerning energy resources allocated to the states *was not obtained*. This action *is needed* so that a determination of redirection *is permitted* on a timely basis when weather conditions change. A system *must be established* so that information on weather conditions and fuel consumption *may be gathered* on a regular basis.

> We *found* that the Department of Energy *did not obtain* information about energy resources that federal offices were allocating to the states. The department *needs* this information so that it *can determine* how to *redirect* these resources when weather conditions change. The secretary of the department *must establish* a system so

that his office *can gather* information on weather conditions and fuel consumption on a regular basis.

The second passage is not only more fluent but also more specific and informative.

To choose between the active and the passive, you can ask yourself two questions: First, must your audience know who is doing what? Often, we deliberately avoid stating who is responsible for an action, either because we don't know or don't care, or because we would rather not say:

> Because the final safety inspection *was* neither *performed* nor *monitored,* the brake plate assembly mechanism *was left* incorrectly aligned, information that *was known* several months before it *was* publicly *revealed.*

More often, though, writers use the passive out of habit, not by design, and so they simply neglect to assign responsibility. In the example about energy, for instance, the writer of the original passage took it for granted that his audience knew who was supposed to be obtaining information, setting up systems, and so on. At other times the real agent is of no importance:

> Between July 2 and July 9, over 5,000 brochures *were printed.*

> If a person is found guilty, he *can be sued* for losses.

> The records *were kept* in a safe.

In sentences like these, the passive is the natural choice.

The second question to ask in choosing active or passive is whether the subjects of your sentences are consistent. If in a series of passive sentences, you find yourself constantly shifting from one subject to another, try rewriting those sentences in the active. If the active version makes those subjects consistent, then make your sentences active.

We should use the beginning of a sentence to orient a reader to what follows. If in a series of sentences we give our reader no consistent starting point, then that stretch of writing will seem less coherent than it might be. Look again at the subjects in the pair of paragraphs about energy. In the first version, the subjects are almost random:

> It . . . information . . . . This action . . . a determination . . . . A
> system . . . information . . . .

In the second, the active sentences provide the reader with a consistent point of view by "staging" the sentences from a consistent set of subject-agents:

> We . . . Department of Energy . . . federal offices . . . . The
> department . . . it . . . . The secretary of the department . . . his
> office . . . .

Each subject anchors the reader in something familiar before he moves on to something new.

On the other hand, when the goal can be made a consistent subject, then the passive is appropriate:

> By the first six months of 1945, it was clear to the world that *the Axis nations* had been essentially defeated, that all that remained was the final, but bloody, climax. The *borders of Germany* had been breached, and *both Germany and Japan* were being bombed around the clock. *Neither country,* though, had been so devastated that it could not resist.

The Institutional Passive

Passives in official and academic prose raise a special problem because prejudice against the first-person *I* or *we* is so widespread. Many writers of scholarly prose, and almost all teachers, believe—mistakenly—that editors will not accept

> After *we irrigated* the peritoneal cavity with saline solution, *we introduced* an acrylic-fiber viewer.

but demand

> After the peritoneal cavity *was irrigated* with saline solution, an acrylic-fiber viewer *was introduced.*

Scientific writing in particular, they believe, demands an aloof, third-person style to demonstrate the author's objectivity—or at least his or her modesty. Yet we have only to glance at some of the best scientific journals to discover instance after instance of *we* as a subject. Here are the first few words from several consecutive sentences in an article in *Science,* a highly prestigious journal:

> . . . we want . . . . Survival gives . . . . We examine . . . . We compare . . . . We have used . . . . Each has been weighted . . . . We merely take . . . . They are subject . . . . We use . . . Efron and Morris (3) describe . . . . We observed . . . . We might find . . . . We know . . . . Averages for a season ordinarily run . . . . Spread comes . . . . We can shrink . . . . How this is done is explained . . . . The explanation is given . . . .
>
> —John P. Gilbert, Bucknam McPeek, and Frederick Mosteller, "Statistics and Ethics in Surgery and Anesthesia," *Science*

This prejudice against first-person writing is as deeply rooted in the academic mentality as it is stylistically unfortunate. Here are two versions of the same content, one passive and thick with nominalizations, the other active and sprinkled with verbs:

> It has been stated that the assessment of the mobility of the detached retina is a factor when the nondrainage retinal detachment operation of Custodis and Lincoff is being given consideration. Determination of the mobility of the detached retina is made on the basis of two factors. The depth of the subretinal fluid is the first to be given consideration. If the subretinal fluid is shallow, then little room is given for actual movement of the detached retina.

> Several researchers have stated that when we consider the Custodis-Lincoff operation in which we do not drain the retina, we must first assess how mobile the detached retina is. We can determine its mobility in two ways. First, how deep is the subretinal fluid? If it is shallow, then the detached retina has little room in which to move.

The active version sounds more prosaic, less academic, the passive version appropriately scientific. But given the choice, who would read page after page of that academic obscurity?

Every profession, of course, demands from its apprentices its own peculiar tone of voice, the special accent that testifies that a writer is familiar with and accepts the implicit values which define that profession. A writer must learn not only to act like a professional but to sound like one as well. It is profoundly unfortunate for us all, but most acutely for the public at large, that the tone most academics assume—unthinkingly or deliberately—makes their prose so resolutely inaccessible.

Of course, we would find most professional prose difficult even if its style were always limpidly clear. To understand advanced work in any field requires that we possess special knowledge, control a technical vocabulary, and understand the nuances of particular forms of argument. But when these problems of local competence conspire with the general problem of an unnecessarily complex prose style, they make it very difficult, if not virtually impossible, for the merely educated and intelligent layperson to appreciate the issues and arguments important not just to a special field, but often to society in general.

Exercise 2-III

Clarify these passages. Change passives into actives only where you think you should. You may have to invent a rhetorical situation in order to explain your choice of active or passive.

1. Your figures have been reanalyzed in order to determine the coefficient of error. The results will be announced when the situation is judged appropriate.
2. Almost all home mortgage loans nowadays are made for twenty-five to thirty years. With the price of housing at such inflated levels, those loans cannot be paid off in any shorter period of time.
3. Trotsky's usual impassioned narrative style is abandoned and in its place a cautious and scholarly treatment of theories of conspiracy is presented. But the moment the narrative line is picked up again, he invests his prose with the same vigor and force.
4. Many arguments have been advanced against Darwinian evolution because basic assumptions about our place in the world were contradicted by it. No longer was man seen as the privileged creature in God's Great Scheme of Things but rather as an accidental consequence of natural forces.
5. For many years federal regulations concerning the use of

wiretapping have been regularly ignored. Only recently have tighter restrictions been imposed on the circumstances that warrant it.

In these next sentences, change passives to actives and edit nominalizations into a more direct agent-action style. Again, invent agents where necessary.

6. It is my belief that the social significance of Restoration comedy can be provided with the clearest explanation through an analysis of social relationships portrayed in the plays. In particular, studies can be made of the manner in which interactions between different social levels are conducted.

7. These technical directives are written in a style of maximum simplicity as a result of an attempt at more effective communication with employees of little education who have been hired in accordance with guidelines that have been imposed.

8. The participants received information that they would be reimbursed, but a decision has been made that such an action cannot be accomplished at this time.

9. The tissue rejection evaluation was performed according to procedures that have been abandoned because of their consistent overestimation of antibody production values.

10. The ability of the human brain to arrive at solutions of human problems has been universally undervalued, because research has not been done that would be considered to have scientific reliability.

SUMMING UP: THE BONES OF A SENTENCE

Passives, nominalizations, compound noun phrases—they all keep us from fully using those resources of an English sentence that can help us express clearly and exactly the meaning we intend. Here are some of the guidelines we've discussed.

1. Whenever you can, use specific verbs, adverbs, or adjectives rather than abstract nouns to express actions and conditions:

The *intention* of this committee is the encouragement of *improvement* in company morale.

This committee *intends* to *improve* company morale.

2. Don't feel constrained to change nominalizations into verbs or adjectives on the following occasions:

   a. The nominalization is close to the end of the sentence or clause and you already have a strong verb:

There is a *need* on our part for your *cooperation*.

We *need* your *cooperation*.

   b. The nominalization sums up an idea in a preceding sentence:

Analyses of this kind invariably produce results that are misleading.

   c. Eliminating a nominalization would require a phrase beginning with *the fact that* or a *what*-clause:

His presence was a factor in *our decision*.

Not: *The fact that he was present* was a factor in *what we decided*.

   d. The nominalization is a common term.

The goal of this *administration* is full *employment* and no *inflation*.

3. Generally, try to make the specific agent of an action the subject. This often means avoiding nominalizations and passives:

A refusal on *your* part to accept the decision will be reviewed *committee*-wise.

If *you* refuse to accept the decision, *the committee* will review your action.

4. Don't feel constrained to change passives into actives under these conditions:

   a. The agent of the action is irrelevant:

When a house *is adequately insulated,* the owner will save money.

   b. The goal of the action is the consistent topic of consecutive clauses:

When *students* are required to take particular courses, *they* sometimes feel as if *they* are being treated like children. And if *they* are so burdened by required courses that *they* cannot choose electives that interest them, *they* can be expected to rebel.

5. Avoid stringing nouns into compound noun phrases:

Teacher evaluation form construction is difficult.

It is difficult to construct forms *for* the evaluation *of* teachers.

Lesson Three

The
Sources of Wordiness

The love of economy is the root of all virtue.

George Bernard Shaw

When we consider the richness, the good sense and strict economy of English, none of the other living languages can be put beside it.

Jacob Grimm

Let thy words be few.

Ecclesiastes 5:2

Loquacity and lying are cousins.

German proverb

Once you learn how to use the grammar of your sentences* to support your ideas, you're a long way toward cleaning up a wordy and indirect style. But some sentences enjoy all the virtues of grammatical clarity yet remain wordy and graceless. Even when you put their grammatical bones in all the right places, they can still succumb to acute prolixity.

> The point I want to make here is that we can see that American policy in regard to foreign countries as the State Department in Washington and the White House have put it together and made it public to the world has given material and moral support to too many foreign factions in other countries that have controlled power and have then had to give up the power to other factions that have defeated them.

That is,

> Our foreign policy has backed too many losers.

In the longer version, the writer matches agents* and actions* to subjects* and verbs*. But he lets his meaning ooze through too many words. He states what he could have left implied; he uses ten words where one would have served.

To write clearly, we have to know not only how to manage the flow of our ideas but also how to prune and compress them. The two principles to keep in mind are easier to state than to follow:

1. Usually, compress what you mean into the fewest words.
2. Don't state what your reader can easily infer.

We plump up our prose in so many ways that it's no use trying to list them all. But you might find it helpful to know the most common kinds of wordiness. This sentence illustrates most of them:

> In my personal opinion, we should basically listen to and think over in a punctilious manner each and every suggestion that is offered to us.

First, opinions can only be personal, so we cut *personal.* And since the whole statement is implicitly opinion, we can cut *in my opinion.* *Basically* means nothing in this sentence, so we cut that too. *Listen to and think over* means *consider,* and *in a punctilious manner* means *punctiliously,* which means no more than *carefully. Each and every* is a redundant pair; we need only *each.* A suggestion is by definition something offered, and offered to someone, so neither do we need *that is offered to us.* What's left is a much leaner,

> We should consider each suggestion carefully.

SOME SIMPLE SOURCES OF WORDINESS

In these cases, you can just cross out words that don't add anything. You don't have to rewrite very much at all.

Redundant Pairs

English has a long tradition of doubled words, a habit that we acquired shortly after we began to borrow from Latin and French the thousands of words that we have since incorporated into English. Because the borrowed word usually sounded a bit more learned than the more familiar native one, early writers would use both. Among the common pairs are *full and complete, true and accurate, hopes and desires, willing and able, hope and trust, each and every, first and foremost, any and all, various and sundry, basic and fundamental, questions and problems,* and, *and so on and so forth.*

Redundant Modifiers

Every word implies another word. *Finish* implies *complete,* so *completely finish* is redundant. *Memories* imply *past,* so *past memories* is redundant. *Different* implies *various,* so *various different* is redundant. *Each* implies *individual,* so *each individual* is redundant. Other examples are such common phrases as *basic fundamentals, true facts, important essentials, future plans, personal beliefs, consensus of opinion, sudden crisis, terrible tragedy, end result, final outcome, initial preparation, free gift.* In every case, we simply prune the redundant modifier. Compare:

> We should not try to anticipate *ahead* those great events that will *completely* revolutionize our society because *past* history tells us that

it has been the *ultimate* effect of little events that has *unexpectedly* surprised us.

We should not try to anticipate those great events that will revolutionize our society because history tells us that it has been the effect of little events that has most surprised us.

Redundant Categories

Specific words imply their general categories, so we usually don't have to state both. We know that time is a period, that the mucous membrane is an area, that pink is a color, and that shiny is an appearance. So we don't have to write,

> During that *period of time,* the *mucous membrane area* became *pink in color* and *of a shiny appearance.*

but only,

> During that *time,* the *mucous membrane* became *pink* and *shiny.*

In some cases, we can eliminate a general category by changing an adjective* into an adverb*:

> The holes must be aligned in an *accurate manner.*

> The holes must be *accurately* aligned.

And in some cases, we can change an adjective into a noun* and drop the redundant noun:

> The *educational process* and *athletic activities* are the responsibility of *county governmental systems.*

> *Education* and *athletics* are the responsibility of *county governments.*

In each case we can delete the general noun and leave the specific word.

Here are some of the common redundant nouns. When you notice any one of these words, see if there is a specific word with it. If there is, you can usually cut the noun:

size, color, weight, taste, shape, form, time, number

appearance, quality, character, condition, state, nature, type, kind, degree, manner, way

process, system, context, activity, factor, action, concept, question, problem, subject, field, area, matter

Meaningless Modifiers

These modifiers are verbal tics that we use almost as unconsciously as we clear our throats. They are words and phrases such as *kind of, really, basically, definitely, practically, actually, virtually, generally, certain, particular, individual, given, various, different, specific, for all intents and purposes.*

> *For all intents and purposes,* American industrial productivity *generally* depends on *certain* factors that are *really* more psychological *in kind* than of any *given* technological aspect.

When we prune both the empty nouns and meaningless modifiers, we have a clearer and sharper,

> American industrial productivity depends more on psychology than technology.

Pompous Diction

Replacing unnecessarily big words with more common ones won't necessarily cut down on the number of words you use, but it will make your diction seem sharper, more direct.

> Pursuant to the recent memorandum issued August 9, 1979, because of petroleum exigencies, it is incumbent upon us all to endeavor to make maximal utilization of telephonic communication in lieu of personal visitation.

means only,

> As the memo of August 9 said, because of the gas shortage, try to use the telephone as much as you can instead of making personal visits.

There is a common word for almost every fancy borrowed one. When we pick the ordinary word over the one that sounds more impressive, we rarely lose anything important, and we gain the simplicity and directness that most effective writing demands.

Sometimes, of course, the more obscure, more formal word is exactly the right one:

> We tried to negotiate in good faith over the additional employee benefits, but the union remains utterly intransigent.

Intransigent is not synonymous with *stubborn* or *firm* or *fixed* or *unyielding* or *uncompromising*. It means to adopt an *unreasonably* fixed position. We can, for example, be uncompromising about our moral behavior, but we would not want to say that we were *intransigent* about it, for that would suggest that we *should* compromise. So if we mean intransigent, then we should use *intransigent*.

More often, though, we choose the big word not for its precision but for its learned weight. Thus the sportscaster who intones,

> His pugilistic exploits supercede even the zenith attained by that memorable and unforgettable nonpareil of athletic endeavor, Sugar Ray Robinson.

or the police officer who reports,

> The alleged felon effectuated entrance into the domicile by means of an appliance forcibly applied to the external locking mechanism.

In a formal situation, most of us choose excessively formal language as a way to compensate for our linguistic insecurity. We can deplore the choice and urge the writer to find a simpler word. But we ought to think twice before we ridicule him. It's a natural impulse that, given the right circumstances, any of us will yield to. You finally have to decide whether a word that feels too big for its sentence *is* too big, or whether it says exactly what you want to say.

A smattering of big words and their more common near-synonyms:

Contingent upon—depend on
Endeavor—try
Utilization—use
Termination—end
Initiate—begin
Is desirous of—wants
Cognizant of—aware of
Ascertain—find out
Facilitate—help
Implement—start, create,
carry out, begin

Deem—think
Envisage—think, regard, see
Avert to—mention
Apprise—inform
Eventuate—happen
Transpire—happen
Render—make
Transmit—send
Prior to—before
Subsequent to—after

Exercise 3-I

Prune the redundancy from these sentences.

1. These various different agencies and offices that provide aid and assistance services to individual persons who participate in our program activities that we offer have reversed themselves back from the policy that they recently announced to return to the original policy that they followed earlier.

2. It is virtually necessary that all critics cannot avoid using and employing complex and abstract terms in order for them to successfully analyze literary textual material and discuss it in a basically meaningful way.

3. The scientific endeavor in general depends on essentially true and fully accurate data if it is to offer any ideas and theories that will actually allow mankind to advance forward into the future in a safe and cautious way.

4. It is probably true that in spite of the fact that the educational environment is a very significant and important facet to each and every one of our children in terms of his or her own individual future development and growth, various different groups and people do not at all support certain tax assessments at a reasonable and fair rate that are required for the express purpose and intention of providing an educational context at a decent level of quality.

5. Most likely, a majority of all the patients who appear at the public medical clinic facility do not expect specialized medical attention and treatment because their health problems and concerns often seem not to be of a major nature and can for the most part usually be adequately treated with enough proper understanding and attention.

SOME COMPLEX KINDS OF WORDINESS

In these cases, you have to think about your prose a bit more carefully; and then rewrite a bit more extensively.

Obvious Implications

Often, we are more diffusely redundant, needlessly stating what we all know.

> Imagine a mental picture of someone engaged in the intellectual activity of trying to learn what the rules are for how to play the game of chess.

Imagine implies a mental picture; *trying to learn* implies being engaged in the activity of; we know chess is intellectual; *chess* implies play, and *play* implies a game. The less redundant version:

> Imagine someone trying to learn the rules of chess.

Or consider this:

> When you write down your ideas, keep in mind that the audience that reads what you have to say to them will infer from your writing style something about your character.

You can write down only ideas; your audience can read only what you have to say; you write only to them; they can infer something about your character only from your writing style. So in fewer words,

> Keep in mind that your audience will infer from your style something about your character.

This kind of redundancy often extends through several sentences, each sentence repeating or implying what has already been stated.

> Today, the period in history known as the Holocaust is alive in the interest of many people. Dozens of films have been made, books written, and TV shows produced recording the events that took place during the Holocaust, describing the various aspects of naziism and the systematic destruction of six million Jews by the Germans under their leader, Adolf Hitler. On the surface, this popular interest in what happened to the Jews under Hitler would appear to be a healthy phenomenon. What could be wrong with a new examination by the media of what is certainly the one single most significant event of twentieth-century history? Unfortunately, this popular interest by so many in the events of the Holocaust has brought with it serious misunderstandings about it, and inevitable incorrect views by those who have been exposed to those misunderstandings.

If we assume that what we say in one sentence doesn't always have to appear in the next, we can make this a good deal leaner and more vigorous:

> Many people have recently become intensely interested in the Holocaust through the dozens of films, books, and TV programs that have dealt with Hitler, naziism, and the Germans' systematic destruction of six million Jews. On the surface, this interest would appear to be healthy: What could be wrong with reexamining the most significant event of the twentieth century? Unfortunately, this interest has also resulted in some serious misunderstandings.

Excessive Detail

Other kinds of redundancy are more difficult to prune. Sometimes, we just provide too many details.

> Baseball, one of our oldest and most popular outdoor summer sports in terms of total attendance at ball parks and viewing on television, has the kind of rhythm of play on the field that alternates between the players' passively waiting with no action taking place between the pitches to the batter and exploding into action when the batter hits a pitched ball to one of the players and he fields it.

That is,

> Baseball has a rhythm that alternates between waiting and explosive action.

How much detail we should provide depends on how much our readers already know. In technical writing, we can usually assume a good deal of shared knowledge.

> The basic type results from simple rearrangement of the phonemic content of polysyllabic forms so that the initial CV of the first stem syllable is transposed with the first CV of the second stem syllable.

The writer didn't bother to define *phonemic content, stem syllable,* or *CV* because he assumed that anyone reading a technical linguistics journal would understand those terms.

On the other hand, this is from an introductory textbook:

> In order to study language scientifically, we need some kind of phonetic transcription, a system to write a language so that visual symbols consistently represent segments of speech.

That definition of *phonetic transcription* would never appear in a technical journal on language, but it's necessary in an introductory textbook.

A Phrase for a Word

The redundancy we've described so far results when we state what could be implied, a problem we can edit away simply by testing the need for every word and phrase. But another kind of redundancy is sometimes more difficult to edit away, because to do so we may need a ready, precise vocabulary and the wit to use it. For example,

> As you carefully read what you have written to improve your wording and catch small errors of spelling, punctuation, and so on, the thing to do before you do anything else is to try to see where sequences of subjects and verbs could replace the same ideas expressed in nouns rather than verbs.

In other words,

> As you edit, first find where you can replace nominalizations with clauses.

We have compressed several words into single words:

carefully read what you have written . . . and so on	=	edit
the thing to do before you do anything else	=	first
try to see where . . . are	=	find
sequences of subjects and verbs	=	clauses
the same ideas expressed in nouns rather than verbs	=	nominalizations

There are no general rules to help you recognize when you can compress several words into a single word or two. I can only point out that you often can do it, and that you should be on the alert for opportunities to do so—try, that is.

You can compress many common phrases:

the reason for	
for the reason that	
due to the fact that	
owing to the fact that	because, since, why
in light of the fact that	
considering the fact that	
on the grounds that	
this is why	

The reason for the success of the program was that we planned it carefully.

The program succeeded *because* we planned it carefully.

In light of the fact that no profits were reported from 1967 through 1974, the stock values remained largely unchanged.

Because no profits were reported from 1967 through 1974, the stock values remained largely unchanged.

It is difficult to explain *the reason for* the delay in the completion of the investigation.

It is difficult to explain *why* we have not yet completed the investigation.

despite the fact that
regardless of the fact that } although, even though
notwithstanding the fact that

Despite the fact that the results were checked several times, serious errors crept into the findings.

Even though the results were checked several times, serious errors crept into the findings.

in the event that
if it should transpire/happen that } if
under circumstances in which

In the event that the materials arrive after the scheduled date, contact the shipping department immediately.

If the materials arrive after the scheduled date, contact the shipping department immediately.

on the occasion of
in a situation in which } when
under circumstances in which

In a situation in which a class is overenrolled, you may request that the instructor reopen the class.

When a class is overenrolled, you may request that the instructor reopen the class.

as regards
in reference to
with regard to } about
concerning the matter of
where _____ is concerned

I should now like to make a few observations *concerning the matter of* contingency funds.

I should now like to make a few observations *about* contingency funds.

it is necessary that
there is a need/necessity for
it is important that   } must
it is incumbent upon
cannot be avoided

There is a need for more careful inspection of all welds.

You *must* inspect all welds more carefully.

Inspect all welds more carefully.

It is important that the proposed North-South Thruway not displace significant numbers of residents.

The proposed North-South Thruway *must* not displace significant numbers of residents.

is able to
has the opportunity to
is in a position to   } can
has the capacity for
has the ability to

We *are in a position to* make you a firm offer for your house.

We *can* make you a firm offer for your house.

it is possible that
there is a chance that   } may, might, can, could
it could happen that
the possibility exists for

It is possible that nothing will come of these preparations.

Nothing *may* come of these preparations.

prior to
in anticipation of
subsequent to   } before, after, as
following on
at the same time as
simultaneously with

Prior to the expiration of the apprenticeship period, it is incumbent upon you that application be made for full membership.

Before your apprenticeship expires, apply for full membership.

Exercise 3-II

Edit these sentences into more economical form.

1. The future that lies before those engaged in studies at the graduate school level and seeking advanced degrees from institutions of higher education in regard to prospects and chances for desirable employment in teaching positions at best does not have a high degree of certainty.
2. Notwithstanding the fact that all legal restrictions on the use of firearms are the subject of heated debate and argument, it is necessary that the general public at large not stop carrying on discussion pro and con in regard to them.
3. Under those circumstances in which individuals with financial resources to invest for a profitable return anticipate the possibility that the continually rising prices of things we buy may continue at steadily increasing rates, those individuals will ordinarily put their financial resources into specific objects of artistic value and worth.
4. In the event that governors of the various states in the United States have the opportunity at some time to get together and talk over with one another the matter of energy needs and problems in their respective states, it is possible that they will find a way to overcome the major problem they have of specifying exactly how to divide up and then distribute to their different states the national supply of fuel resources intended for motor vehicle use.
5. Those people who in times past established our particular form of government never thought about the future in regard to how those whose business it is to influence the people we elect to pass laws would make those we elect do what they want them to do, due to the fact that none of those original founders were in a position to realize the degree to which business enterprises could achieve excessive size and great power.
6. The most major matter I want to ask about at this point is the degree to which the consciousness that writers have about the individuals they create in their plays puts a disguise on the social tensions of the times in which they are writing.
7. Those engaged in the profession of education and teaching have for a long period of time been interested in having a better

idea about and making significant improvements in how different individuals learn and commit to memory any and all information from given written textual material. The first matter of difficulty is identifying aspects of common and different features among comparable stretches of textual writing. The second addresses the difficult matter of assigning some kind of value to the amount of and nature of information that a reader does not forget after that person reads a passage of writing.

TALKING TO THE READER: METADISCOURSE

Whenever we write more than a few words, we usually have to write on two levels. We write about the subject we are addressing, of course: foreign policy, falling sales, the operation of a computer system. But we also directly or indirectly tell our audience how they should take our ideas. In those last two sentences, for example, *of course, but,* and *also* serve more to direct you than to inform you. And in that last sentence, *for example* told you how to connect the sentence to the previous two.

We could use a term to distinguish this kind of writing that guides the reader, from writing that informs the reader about primary topics: We'll call it *metadiscourse**, discourse about discoursing. We need some metadiscourse in just about everything we write. Without it, we couldn't announce that we're changing the subject or coming to a conclusion, that what we're asserting is or is not certain, that our ideas are important. We couldn't define terms or acknowledge a difficult line of thought, or even note the existence of a reader.

We use a good deal of metadiscourse in personal narratives, arguments, memoirs—any discourse in which we filter our ideas through a concern with how our reader will take them. Except for numbers to indicate sections and so on, other kinds of writing—operating instructions, technical manuals, laws, and the like—can be relatively free of metadiscourse.

The problem is to recognize when metadiscourse is useful and then to learn how to control it. Some writers use so much metadiscourse that they bury their primary message. For example,

The last point I would like to make here is that in regard to
men-women relationships, it is important to keep in mind that the
greatest changes have in all probability occurred in the way men
and women seem to be working next to one another.

Only part of that sentence addresses men-women relationships:

> . . . men-women relationships . . . greatest changes have . . .
> occurred in the way men and women . . . working next to one
> another.

The rest tells readers how to understand what they are reading:

> The last point I would like to make here is that in regard to . . . it
> is important to keep in mind that . . . in all probability . . . seem
> to . . . .

Pruned of this writing about reading, the sentence becomes a good
bit more direct:

> The greatest changes in men-women relationships have occurred
> in the way men and women work next to one another.

And now that we can see what this sentence really says, we can make
it even more direct:

> Relationships between men and women have changed most in the
> way they work together.

In deciding how much metadiscourse to include, we can't rely on
any large generalizations. Some entirely successful writers use a
good deal of metadiscourse; others equally successful, very little.
More often than not, though, it can be cut. Of course, read widely
in your field with an eye to how writers you think are clear, concise,
and successful use metadiscourse. Then do as they do.

Here are some of the more common types of metadiscourse.

Hedges and Emphatics

Each profession has its own idiom of caution and confidence. None
of us wants to sound like an uncertain milquetoast or a smug
dogmatist. How successfully we tread the rhetorical line between

seeming timidity and arrogance depends a good deal on how we manage phrases like *a good deal,* a phrase that a few words ago allowed me to pull back from the more absolute statement,

> How successfully we tread the rhetorical line between seeming timidity and arrogance depends on how we manage phrases like a *a good deal.*

Hedges let us sound small notes of civilized diffidence. They leave us room for backpedaling and making exceptions. An appropriate emphatic, on the other hand, lets us underscore what we really believe—or would like our reader to think we believe.

Some of the more common hedges: *usually, often, sometimes, almost, virtually, possibly, perhaps, apparently, seemingly, in some ways, to a certain extent, sort of, for the most part, for all intents and purposes, in some respects, in my opinion at least, may, might, can, could, seem, tend, try, attempt, seek, hope.* Some of us use these so often that they become less hedges than meaningless modifiers.

Some of the more common emphatics: *as everyone knows, it is generally agreed that, it is quite true that, it's clear that, the fact is, as we can plainly see, literally, clearly, obviously, undoubtedly, certainly, of course, indeed, inevitably, very, invariably, always, key, central, crucial, basic, fundamental, major, cardinal, primary, principal, essential, integral.* Words and phrases like these generally mean "believe me" and not much .more. Used to excess, they sound arrogant, or at least defensive. Or they become a kind of distracting background static that robs a style of any clarity or precision. This is another case where a good ear will serve you better than a flat rule.

Sequencers and Topicalizers

These are words that lead your reader through your text. I'll say more about them when we discuss how to make a discourse cohesive, how to carry a reader easily from one sentence to the next. I mention them here because they can obscure what a writer says as easily as they can help clarify it.

The least useful kind of sequencers are those overelaborate introductions:

> In this next section of this report, it is my intention to deal with the problem of noise pollution. The first thing I want to say about this subject is this: Noise pollution is . . .

You can usually announce the topic* of a whole discourse—or any of its parts—and hint at the structure of its argument much more simply:

> The next problem is noise pollution. It . . .

Unless you require an elaborate introduction that specifically lays out the plan of your paper, assume that just naming the problem is sufficient to announce it as your topic.

Specific topicalizers focus attention on a particular phrase as the main topic of a sentence, paragraph, or whole section:

> *In regard to a vigorous style,* the most important characteristic is a short, concrete subject followed by a forceful verb.

> *Where the industrial development of China is concerned,* it will be years before it becomes competitive with Japan's.

> *As to the matter of responsibility for security,* that is the problem of the building and grounds staff.

We use phrases and clauses such as *in regard to, where X is concerned, in the matter of, as for, as to, speaking of, turning now to,* and so on to announce that we are moving on to a new idea. But consider whether you can maneuver that new idea into the body of the sentence.

> *The most important characteristic of a vigorous style* is a short, concrete subject followed by a forceful verb.

> It will be years before China's *industrialization* becomes competitive with Japan's.

> *Responsibility for security* belongs to the building and grounds staff.

Probably the most common topicalizer is *there is/are.*

> There are three reasons why we should recognize Outer Mongolia.

There is/are often occurs at the beginning of a section, announcing in the phrase that follows *is/are* the topic of that section. But whatever follows *there is/are* is always a noun phrase*, always static. So use this construction only when that phrase is important enough to develop in the next few sentences. Too many *there is/are*s simply present a series of topics, eventually retarding the flow of a paragraph. Compare:

> *There is* no easy way to resolve this conflict between the rich and the poor nations of the earth. *There is* a need for a greater altruism than we in the northern European countries now display, if *there is* to be an equitable distribution of the world's increasingly scarce resources and energy. And unless *there is* a solution to the problem, *there will be* a worldwide explosion into economic and racial warfare.

> We shall find no easy way to resolve this conflict between the rich and the poor nations of the earth. We in the northern European countries will have to act more altruistically than we have if we are to distribute equitably the world's increasingly scarce resources and energy. And unless we solve this problem, the world will explode into economic and racial warfare.

Attributors and Narrators

These are words that tell your reader where your ideas or facts or opinions came from. Sometimes, when we are still trying to work out precisely what it is we want to say, we offer a narrative of our thinking rather than its results:

> *I was concerned with* the structural integrity of the roof supports, so *I attempted* to test the weight that the transverse beams would carry. *I have concluded* after numerous tests that the beams are sufficiently strong to carry the prescribed weight, but no more. *I think* that it is important that we notify every section that uses the facility of this finding.

If we eliminate the narrators and refocus our attention on what the reader needs to know, we can make the passage a good deal more pointed:

> We must notify every section that uses the storage facility that they must not exceed the prescribed kilogram-per-square-meter floor weight. Tests have established the structural integrity of the transverse beams. They are strong enough to carry the prescribed weights but no more than that.

Unless the topic of your discourse must be the process by which you arrived at your observations or conclusion, you can usually be more concise and direct if you simply present the most salient observations and conclusions, minus the metadiscourse or narrative.

Some writers slip this kind of attribution into their prose more indirectly, by stating that something has been *observed* to exist, is *found* to exist, is *seen, noticed, noted, remarked,* etc.

> High divorce rates *have been observed to occur* in parts of the Northeast that *have been determined to have* especially low population densities.

> Regular patterns of drought and precipitation *have been found to coincide* with cycles of sunspot activity.

Unless you have some good reason to hedge a bit, leave out the fact that any unspecified observer has *observed, found, noticed,* or *seen* something. Just state that it is:

> High divorce rates *occur* in parts of the Northeast that *have* especially low population densities.

> Regular patterns of drought and precipitation *coincide* with cycles of sunspot activity.

If this seems too flat–footed, drop in a hedge: . . . *apparently coincide.*

Exercise 3-III

In these next sentences, edit for both unnecessary metadiscourse and redundancy.

1. But on the other hand, however, in opposition to this, we can point out that it appears more and more certainly the case that there is going to continue to be TV programming that will on the whole appeal to what can only be considered our most prurient and, therefore, lowest interests.

2. A definition of the term *seborrhea* may be formulated by one in the following general way: By *seborrhea* we basically refer to an accumulation and buildup on the surface area of the skin of what would not be diagnosed as normal or

usual sebacious secreted matter, with creation of scab formations or encrustations.

3. It may possibly turn out to be the situation that the playwright known to us by the name of William Shakespeare could be someone else; perhaps someone whom we would find to be a member of royalty.

4. In this particular section, I intend to discuss my feelings about the need not to continue with the old approach to plea bargaining. I believe this is the case because of two basic reasons. The first reason that it is necessary to deal with plea bargaining is that it appears to let hardened criminals not receive their just punishment. The second reason is the following one: plea bargaining virtually always encourages a growing lack of respect for the judicial system.

5. In conclusion, I would like to point out that in regard to China, it appears to be a good example of a country on the verge of what many observers agree is going to be what could only be called a major industrial expansion.

6. Turning now to the next question to be discussed and considered here, there are in regard to the subject of wild area preservation activities three basic principles that can be stated when attempting to formulate a way of approaching decisions as to those wild and uninhabited areas unspoiled by human activity that should be set aside and preserved and not developed for commercial exploitation or business enterprises.

7. It is my underlying belief that in regard to terrestial-type snakes, the assumption can safely be made and followed that there are in all probability none to speak of in those unmapped portions or areas of the world not yet explored that would be in excess to any significant degree of the size of those we already have knowledge of.

8. As far as I am concerned, I think that in light of the fact that Leon Trotsky was clearly and distinctly in favor of the Communist Revolution and overthrow of the Tsar, there is no possibility of arguing that he would ever be in a position to have an objective viewpoint in regard to those events.

9. It seems to me that Imagism appears to mimic the haiku's use of strong visual patterns to provoke feelings and

emotions at the same time that it does not accept the idea that any particular image and particular emotion require what we would take to be traditional correspondences.

10. As we can see, I think that in regard to the current interest in life stages, it would appear that most investigators into the subject area have a tendency to take the position that the midlife crisis is in all probability the most critical period or stage in a person's life development from a mental health point of view; that is to say, we are in a position to know that for the most part, a large number of us seem to come to the decision at that particular time in our lives whether or not we are going to be what we might wish to call those on the winning or losing side of the game of life.

NOT THE NEGATIVE

For all practical purposes, these two sentences mean about the same thing:

> Don't write in the negative.

> Write in the affirmative.

But if we want to be utterly concise and straightforward, we ought to prefer the more direct.

> Write in the affirmative.

To understand the negative, we have to translate it into an affirmative, because the negative only *implies* what we should do by telling us what we shouldn't do. The affirmative *states* it directly. Compare what you just read with this:

> "Don't write in the negative" and "Write in the affirmative" *do not mean* different things. But if *we don't want* to be indirect, then we *should not prefer* "Don't write in the negative." *We don't have to translate* an affirmative statement *in order not to misunderstand* it because it *does not imply* what we should do.

Of course, we can't easily translate every negative sentence into an affirmative. But we can rephrase many negatives as affirmatives, and unless you have some special reason to emphasize a *not, no,* or *never,* look for that affirmative sentence.

Some negatives allow almost formulaic translations into affirmatives:

not many ⟶ *few*
not the same ⟶ *different*
not different ⟶ *alike/similar*
did not ⟶ *failed to*
does not have ⟶ *lacks*
did not stay ⟶ *left*
not old enough ⟶ *too young*
did not remember ⟶ *forgot*
did not consider ⟶ *ignored*
did not have anything to do with ⟶ *avoided*
did not allow ⟶ *prevented*
did not accept ⟶ *rejected*
not clearly ⟶ *unclearly*
not possible ⟶ *impossible*
not able ⟶ *unable*
not certain ⟶ *uncertain*

Now certainly, this advice does not apply to those sentences that raise an issue by contradicting or denying some point that we intend to correct (as this sentence demonstrates). One of the most common ways we introduce a chunk of discourse is to deny, to say "not so" to someone else's idea of the truth, or even some possible truth. Once we deny it, we then go on to assert the truth as we see it:

> In the last decade of the 20th century, we will not find within our own borders sufficient oil to meet our needs, nor will we find it in the world market. The only way we will increase our oil supply is by developing the one resource that we have so far ignored: massive conservation.

A FINE POINT: Directing Directly

When you combine negatives with passives*, nominalizations*, and compounds* in sentences that are already a bit complex, you can become virtually opaque:

> Disengagement of the gears is not possible without locking
> mechanism release.

> Payments should not be forwarded if there has not been due
> notification of this office.

These particular negatives all involve two events, one a precondition
of the other. We can always recast such negatives into more direct
affirmatives if we change nominalizations into clauses and passives
into actives.

> If you want to disengage the gears, you must first release the
> locking mechanism.

> Before you forward any payments, notify this office.

And be especially careful when you combine outright negatives
like *no, not,* and *never* with verbs and prepositions that imply a
negative: *avoid, fail, lack, doubt, reject, preclude, deny, except, without.*
Whether you put the necessary precondition of the desired
outcome first depends on matters we'll take up more fully in Lesson
6. In brief, the principle is this: What is it that the readers are looking
for, want to do, want done? It's how to disengage gears, when to
forward payments. Put that first. That's the result the readers are
looking for or the knowledge they already have. That's the point
they will most quickly identify. Put last the new information that
you are giving to your readers, the information that they do not yet
have.

> Benefits will not be denied except when applicants have submitted
> applications without appropriate documentation.

> You will receive your benefits only if you submit appropriate
> documents when you apply.

Exercise 3-IV

Where appropriate, change the following to affirmatives. Do any
additional editing you think useful.

1. It is not possible to reduce inflationary pressures when the
   federal government does not reduce its spending.
2. Sufficient research has not been directed to the problems of

individuals who cannot see when there are not normal levels of light.

3. Scientists have not agreed on the question of whether the universe is open or closed, a dispute that will not be resolved until the total mass of the universe has been computed with an error of no more than 5 percent.

4. So long as taxpayers do not refuse to pay their taxes, the government will have no difficulty in paying its debts.

5. We have no alternative to developing tar sand, oil shale, and coal as sources of fuel, because we cannot make ourselves vulnerable to foreign powers that at any moment might not continue to supply us with oil.

6. There has not been adequate carcinogen prevention established in the chemical additive area of meat production.

7. Cancerous tumor treatment is not effective if growth removal is not accomplished before tumor metastasis.

8. Not until a resolution between Catholics and Protestants in regard to papal authority supremacy is achieved will there be the beginning of a reconciliation between the two.

9. Elections in which there is no attempt at dealing with those issues which do not receive adequate attention during the time when no election campaigns are under way cannot serve the functions for which they were intended.

10. The Insured may not refuse to provide the Insurer with all relevant receipts, checks, or other evidence of costs except when such expenses do not exceed $110.

11. Do not discontinue medication unless symptoms of dizziness and nausea fail to alleviate within six hours.

12. The lack of disconfirming evidence suggests that the results are not open to dispute, unless the absence of data from other investigations is taken as a negative factor.

13. No one is precluded from participating in the cost-sharing educational programs without a full hearing into the reasons for his or her rejection.

14. Because there have been no violations of the guidelines by HEW-supported public agencies, there appears to be no reason for the rejection of their application. The conclusion that such action was a result of political pressure cannot be avoided.

Now go back to exercises I–III and look for negatives that you can change to affirmatives.

Exercise 3-V

Edit the redundancy out of these sentences. Where appropriate change negatives to affirmatives.

1. It seems to me that in a systematic look at the nature of advertising, it is not illogical and unreasonable to start out with a statement that will define the term. This will establish a common shared point of reference so that we will not be subjective in our approach to the subject matter that is not often the topic of unemotional discussion. Unfortunately there is no single definition for the word *advertising,* making the chances for possible objectivity not likely. This indicates that the generally popular notions about advertising cannot be examined carelessly.
2. Regardless of the apparent fact that we do not know for certain whether or not there is any possibility in regard to the existence of what we would think were life forms in different parts of the universe other than the one in which we exist, it seems to be probable that evidence that cannot be refuted that is of a basically statistical kind makes it appear that it is highly unlikely that life could not be found in a large number of planetary systems around tens of thousands of stars scattered throughout the length and the breadth of the universe as we know it.

SUMMING UP: CUTTING FAT

You can cut verbal fat if you get rid of the kind of abstraction we discussed in Lesson 2. But you can also make your style leaner and more direct if you clear away the more diffuse kind of wordiness we've discussed in this lesson. Unfortunately, I can't offer any strong generalizations to equal those I suggested about making subjects coincide with agents, verbs with actions. Diffuse wordiness is more like a chronic accumulation of specks and motes that individually may seem trivial but together blur what might otherwise be a clear and concise style.

Here again is a list of the problems, along with examples and revisions.

1. *Redundant pairs*

If and when we can define and establish our final aims and goals, each and every member of our group will be ready and willing to offer aid and assistance.

If we can define our goals, every member of our group will be ready to offer assistance.

2. *Redundant modifiers*

In this world of today, official governmental red tape is seriously destroying initiative among individual business executives.

Today, government red tape is destroying initiative among business executives.

3. *Redundant categories*

In the area of educational activities, tight financial conditions are forcing school board members to cut back in nonessential areas in a drastic manner.

In education, tight finances are forcing school boards to cut back drastically on nonessentials.

4. *Meaningless modifiers*

Most students generally find some kind of summer work.

Most students find summer work.

5. *Obvious implications*

Energy used to power our industries and homes will in the years to come be increasingly expensive in terms of dollars and cents.

In the future, energy will cost more.

6. *Pompous diction*

You must endeavor to facilitate their cognizance of the deleterious result of excessive sesquipedalianism.

You have to help them realize that big words can have bad results.

7. *Excessive detail*

A microwave oven that you might buy in any department store uses less energy that is so expensive than a conventional oven that uses gas.

Microwave ovens use less energy than conventional ovens.

8. *A Phrase for a word*

A small sail-powered craft that has turned on its side or completely over must remain buoyant enough so that it will bear the weight of those individuals who were aboard.

A small sailboat that capsizes must float well enough to support its crew.

9. *Excessive metadiscourse*

It is almost certainly the case that, for the most part, totalitarian systems cannot allow a society to settle into what we would perceive to be stable modes of behavior or, even more crucially perhaps, stable relationships.

Totalitarian systems cannot allow a society to settle into stable behavior or stable relationships.

10. *Indirect negatives*

There is no reason not to believe that engineering malfunctions in nuclear energy systems cannot always be anticipated.

We can assume that malfunctions in nuclear energy systems will surprise us.

It's not necessary to memorize these types of redundancy, or even unfailingly distinguish one from another. What is important is an eye—or an ear—for a loose phrase, for a useless modifier, for that haze of wordiness that can afflict the prose of even the best writers when they become inattentive.

Lesson Four

Controlling Sprawl

Then said I, Lord, how long.

Isaiah 6:11

Too much of a good thing is worse than none at all.

English proverb

Too much noise deafens us; too much light dazzles us; too much distance or too much proximity impedes vision; too much length or too much brevity of discourse obscures it . . . .

Blaise Pascal

Once you've squeezed the fat out of a sentence* and matched your ideas to its grammatical structure (and vice versa), you've often solved the third most common problem that makes for hard reading: disorganized sprawl. When a reader begins to feel that a sentence is never going to end, when its sprawling length has exhausted his attention, he will simply quit on you. By cutting away excess verbiage and useless abstraction, you make your sentences shorter and crisper. But sometimes, even when you've expressed your ideas directly and economically, you can still lose a reader if you've packed too many ideas into a single unbroken sentence:

> Now that the flower children of the '60s have grown up to become the industrial and service workers of the '70s, employers have discovered that they must learn how to motivate a new kind of worker who rejects the values of older workers for whom a job is a means to status and affluence and instead looks upon labor as a necessary evil that he will endure only if he receives a high salary, generous fringe benefits, and several weeks of paid vacation.

Straightforward and direct, perhaps, but far too long to be clear. Compare:

> Now that the flower children of the '60s have grown up to become the industrial and service workers of the '70s, employers have discovered that they must learn how to motivate a new kind of worker. These younger employees have rejected the values of older workers, for whom a job was a means to status and affluence. Our younger workers look upon labor as a necessary evil that they will endure only if they receive high salaries, generous fringe benefits, and several weeks of paid vacation.

TWO KINDS OF SENTENCES

We have to distinguish two kinds of long sentences; the one you're reading right now, for example, is rather long, sixty-four words to be exact, but it's long because I have simply chosen to punctuate what might have been a series of shorter sentences as one long sentence; those semicolons could have been periods—and that dash could have been one too.

But I can write a different sentence that is just as long as that, but one that doesn't let me trade a comma, semicolon, or dash for a period, because it is composed of several subordinate parts, all depending on a single main clause*—indeed a sentence such as the one you are now reading, which is also exactly sixty-four words long.

Both of those sentences were single *punctuated sentences,* stretches that began with a capital letter and ended with a period. But the first consisted of shorter segments, shorter coordinated* clauses* that could have been punctuated as separate sentences, like this slightly revised version:

> We have to distinguish two kinds of long sentences. The one you're reading right now, however, is rather short, sixteen words to be exact. But it's short because I have simply chosen to punctuate what might have been one long sentence as a series of shorter ones. Those periods could have been semicolons. And that period could have been a dash.

Traditionally, we use the term *compound sentence** to describe punctuated sentences that link clause to clause with semicolons or with coordinating conjunctions* such as *and, but, yet, for, so, or* or *nor.* More than two or three such clauses in a single punctuated sentence risks creating a kind of breathless tumbling of ideas:

> Language was one of the great evolutionary breakthroughs in our species, *and* it probably made possible the domination of a large food-providing area by a relatively few creatures, *and* it may even have enhanced selection for intellectual power, *but* without the equally important ability to use tools, we never would have survived, *so* it is important that we analyze our evolution in both these contexts, *and* that is what this chapter will do.

Even though that is a very long punctuated sentence, it is made up of several very short and simple *grammatical sentences.*

A grammatical sentence, as we will use the term here, is a sentence that we cannot break into two shorter sentences with just a period, no matter how long it is. Traditionally, we call these either *simple sentences,* sentences with a single clause:

> The source of certain knowledge always puzzled Socrates.

or *complex sentences,* sentences with an independent clause and at least one subordinate clause*:

> [Although there are many great dictionaries,] the greatest dictionary of them all is the *Oxford English Dictionary.*

Neither of those example sentences can be broken into two smaller sentences. When we do break a single grammatical sentence into two punctuated sentences incorrectly (as I am about to do). We have what is called a fragment. Such as the one that began *When we do break* and the one you're reading right now. Here's how those fragments should have been punctuated (again, slightly revised):

> Neither of those sentences can we break into two smaller sentences, as that comma testifies. When we do break a single grammatical sentence into two punctuated sentences inappropriately, we have what is called a *fragment,* such as the one that began *When we do break,* but not the sentence you're reading now.

Keep this principle in mind: If a very long *punctuated* sentence is a single *grammatical* sentence, it may be difficult to read because it gives a reader no place to pause and begin again. On the other hand, if a very long punctuated sentence consists of several short grammatical sentences, it may be simple to read, but it may also sound a bit childish.

THE BEST LENGTH

We can think about how long a sentence ought to be in two ways. First, we could aim at the norm for different kinds of prose. In ordinary magazine writing, for example, sentences average about twenty to twenty-two words. In more technical and academic prose, they are considerably longer. In writing aimed at a very general reading public, newspaper writing for example, sentences are shorter.

The better way to think about length is to develop a sense for when a sentence is going on too long. In practice, a grammatical sentence usually becomes too long when a writer tacks on to one clause another that modifies it, and to that clause, yet one more:

The function of myth is to tell a story *that* will allow an interpretation *that* speaks to some problem basic to the society of its audience *because* myth is a kind of history *that* orders the world for preliterates for *whom* abstract moral or social philosophy would be irrelevant.

That's another kind of sprawl: not several sentences within a single punctuated sentence, but a single grammatical sentence that wanders through one tacked-on dependent, subordinate clause after another.

As a first step toward sensing when your sentences begin to sprawl, find out roughly how long they run./The easiest way to find out is to put a slash mark at every period and inside every punctuated sentence where a grammatical sentence ends;/a grammatical sentence ended there, for example, and ends here./If you know roughly how many words a line of your typed or written copy averages—usually ten to fourteen—then you can tell at a glance about how many words you average per sentence./Since that one ran about three typed lines, I guess it was about thirty-three to thirty-six words long, close enough for our purposes.

If most of your sentences run more than two-and-a-half lines, you may be plain wordy, or you may be trying to pack too much into your sentences. And as a result, you may be asking too much of your readers.

CUTTING DOWN LONG SENTENCES

The simplest way to edit sprawling sentences, particularly long punctuated sentences with lots of *and*s or *but*s, is simply to stop them with a period and delete the unnecessary conjunctions*. Compare this with the original version on page 63:

Language was one of the great evolutionary breakthroughs in our species: It probably made possible the domination of a large food-providing area by a relatively few creatures; it may even have enhanced selection for intellectual power. But without the equally important ability to use tools, we never would have survived. It is important that we analyze our evolution in both these contexts. That is what this chapter will do.

Because *and* usually just means "Here's one more thing," you can usually drop *and*. You can also drop most *sos*. If you find that you cannot, the flow of your argument may need some attention: Logical conclusions should be obvious from what preceded them.

Ordinarily, you can't omit a *but* or *yet*. You have to signal qualifications and contradictions. When we remove the *but*, the sentence beginning with *Without* seems disjointed:

> Language was one of the great evolutionary breakthroughs in our species. It probably made possible the domination of a large food-providing area by a relatively few creatures; it may even have enhanced selection for intellectual power. Without the equally important ability to use tools, we never would have survived. It is important that we analyze our evolution in both these contexts. That is what this chapter will do.

As a general rule, if a clause beginning with *but* or *and* introduces a major point that you intend to develop, punctuate that clause as a separate sentence:

> We must acknowledge that the United States government has a long history of broken treaties with the Indian nations *that trusted it, but it is equally true* that in recent history, it has attempted to redress many of those broken agreements. In Maine, for example, the federal government has . . .

Beginning a new sentence at *But it is equally true* makes the thesis more prominent:

> We must acknowledge that the United States government has a long history of broken treaties with the Indian nations *that trusted it. But it is equally true* that in recent history, it has attempted to redress many of those broken agreements. In Maine, for example, . . .

However, when the clauses are short and the *but*-clause is closely tied to the preceding clause, you gain little except special emphasis by splitting them with a period:

> Prices are *going up, but wages* are going up a bit faster.

> Prices are *going up. But wages* are going up a bit faster.

While long sentences containing several grammatical sentences can simply be repunctuated, splitting up long grammatical sentences takes a bit of rewriting. Here are some ways to do it.

Splitting before an **And**

If the sentence contains two long coordinate verb phrases*, put a period before the *and* or *but* and find a subject* for the second verb phrase.

> Students of animal behavior *have been concerned* with the problem of the sensory control of motivation and emotion during periods of unusual stress *and have studied* the behavior of many species under controlled conditions of various kinds.

> Students of animal behavior *have been concerned* with the problem of the sensory control of motivation and emotion during periods of unusual stress. *They have studied* the behavior of many species under controlled conditions of various kinds.

Splitting If/when/though/because-clauses

In these cases, we turn a subordinate clause into an independent clause. The most convenient place to break a single long grammatical sentence is usually just before or after a dependent clause beginning with *because, if, although, when, since, while, before,* and so on. But you'll have to replace that *because, when, although, if,* etc., with a new sentence connector. In the following sentences, we replace the subordinating conjunctions with *but, so, if so,* and so on.

> (a) *while, although, though* ⟶ *but, yet, however*

> *Although* the court ordered the police to remain on the job until the injunction against the strike had been rescinded by a higher court, they refused the order and went out on strike regardless of the penalties that they knew would be levied against them.

> The court ordered the police to remain on the job until the injunction against the strike had been rescinded by a higher court. *But* they refused the order and went out on strike . . . .

> (b) *because, since* ⟶ *as a result, consequently, as a consequence,*
> *because of this, so*

How you split cause and effect sentences linked with *because* or *since* is more complicated. It depends on what comes first—the cause or the effect. If the cause comes first, you can introduce the effect with *as a result, consequently,* etc.

> *Because* the American labor force is changing from a manufacturing to a service force that cannot be as easily unionized as the large industrial complexes of the 1930s and '40s, organized labor has lost a good deal of the political power it once used to elect candidates who supported their goals.

> The American labor force is changing from a manufacturing to a service force that cannot be as easily unionized as the large industrial complexes of the 1930s and '40s. *As a result,* organized labor has lost a good deal of the political power . . . .

But if the effect comes first and the cause second, then we have to introduce the cause with *this happened because, this occurred because, we did this because,* etc.

> Organized labor has lost a good deal of the political power it once used to elect candidates who supported *its goals* **because** *the American labor force* is changing from a manufacturing to a service force that cannot be as easily unionized as the large industrial complexes of the 1930s and '40s.

> Organized labor has lost a good deal of the political power it once used to elect candidates who supported *its goals. This has* **happened** **because** *the American labor force* is changing from a manufacturing . . . .

(c) *if, provided that,* ⟶ *if so, if this is so, if this happens*

> **If** demographic changes continue as they have over the last several years, shrinking the future working population by as much *as 25 percent, we may find* it difficult to go on supporting a relatively large elderly population on the taxed earnings of a relatively small labor force.

> Demographic changes could continue as they have over the last several years, shrinking the future working population by as much *as 25 percent. If this happens, we may find* it difficult to go on supporting a relatively large elderly population on the taxed earnings of a relatively small labor force.

Splitting before a Which/who/that-clause

A string of relative clauses is invariably limp and graceless. We can correct it simply by cutting the string at some appropriate place.

It is easy to understand why special interest laws are so attractive to *lawmakers **who** have to share* credit with hundreds of other legislators **who** pass broadly based laws **that** benefit everyone but can enjoy the special thanks **that** special groups can offer for successful advocacy of special laws.

It is easy to understand why special interest laws are so attractive to *lawmakers*. *They* have to share credit with hundreds of other legislators who pass broadly based laws that benefit *everyone*. *But lawmakers* can enjoy the special thanks that special interest groups can offer for successful advocacy of special laws.

When *which* refers to the whole of the previous clause, find a word that will replace the *which* and begin a new sentence.

Mapmaking in Europe entered a renaissance in both theory and practice during the sixteenth and seventeenth centuries, *which* was the result of exploration and colonization of the New World and commercial relations with Asia.

Mapmaking in Europe entered a renaissance in both theory and practice during the sixteenth and seventeenth centuries. *This development* resulted from the exploration and colonization of the New World and from commercial relations with Asia.

Splitting with a Colon

If a sentence contains a long list, you can help the reader if you place a colon before it. But remember that you ought to have a complete sentence ***before*** the colon.

In order to analyze the structural properties of discourse, it is necessary *to account for: the flow of semantic* information in a paragraph, the devices used to achieve coherence, and the functional units in paragraphs such as topic sentences.

In order to analyze the structural properties of discourse, it is necessary to account *for the following: the flow of semantic* information in a paragraph, the devices. . . .

(Note: Most handbooks recommend beginning the section after a colon with a lower-case letter. If what follows the colon is not a complete clause, you can still begin with the lower-case letter. But if you have finished one clause and are beginning another complete clause, you can signal that fact to your reader by beginning that next clause with a capital letter: This clause is an example.)

SOME FINE POINTS: Managing Connections

1. *Although*———*but*. • *Although* and *but* indicate qualifications in different ways. When we read a sentence that begins with *although*, we have to keep in mind that the first idea is going to be contradicted or qualified by what follows it. But [as in this case] when the contradiction is signaled with a *but* or *however* at the beginning of the second idea, we have to recall what we just read to make sense of the contradiction or qualification.

> *Although* [the reader must anticipate] legalized gambling is potentially a rich source of revenue, it can create serious social problems.

> Legalized gambling is potentially a rich source of revenue, *but* [the reader must recall] it can create serious social problems.

This is one reason why connectives such as *however, nevertheless,* and *on the other hand* ought to appear somewhere close to the beginning of their sentence. The second sentence here seems to reverse itself very abruptly at the end.

> Legalized gambling is potentially a rich source of tax revenue. It has proven in practice to be a source of serious social problems, *however.*

When an *although*-clause occurs at the end of a sentence, it can sound like a tacked-on afterthought.

> Legalized gambling can create serious social problems, *although* it is potentially a rich source of tax revenue.

If the next sentence picks up on the tax revenue, then make that last clause about revenue a *main* clause, leading into the next sentence.

Although legalized gambling can create serious social problems, it is potentially a rich source of tax revenue. Both Nevada and New Jersey have realized several millions of dollars . . . .

If instead the next sentence picks up on the social problems, then make the clause about problems the main clause, and put it at the end, so that it leads into that next sentence.

Although legalized gambling is potentially a rich source of tax revenue, it can also create serious social problems. Communities in which such gambling is allowed have experienced sharp increases in prostitution, robbery, loan sharking. . . .

An *even though* is more emphatic than a simple *although,* and can make its clause strong enough to stand at the end without seeming anticlimactic.

Legalized gambling is potentially a rich source of tax revenues, *even though* it carries with it social risks that we might not want to take.

2. *Because* ⟶ *as a result.* • When you break up a sentence that begins with a *because-* or *since-*clause, start the second sentence with *as a result.* Do not use *this had the result of, this resulted in, this led to,* or *this had the effect of.* The prepositions* at the end of those phrases will force you into awkward nominalizations* and their attendant prepositional phrases. Compare this first passage with a *because* and the second with a *this has resulted in:*

Because the soaring cost of energy, the single most important factor in the economy of the late twentieth century, has shaken the confidence of the world in our ability to sustain a healthy rate of growth, foreign investors have lost confidence in the dollar as a secure form of financial reserve.

The soaring cost of energy, the single most important factor in the economy of the late twentieth century, has shaken the confidence of the world in our ability to sustain a healthy rate of growth. *This has resulted in a loss of confidence* by foreign investors. . . .

Now compare phrases such as *as a result, consequently, as a consequence,* or *because of this,* that let you state an effect with the verb* expressing the crucial action:

. . . a healthy rate of growth. *As a result,* foreign investors have *lost* confidence in the dollar. . . .

When we write a sentence that begins with the effect and ends with a *since-* or *because*-clause (the cause), we have a bit more difficulty in splitting it up gracefully. English doesn't have an idiomatic connective parallel to *therefore* or *as a result* to signal that the second clause is a cause. *For* will occasionally serve:

> Many of our older cities are facing fiscal crises far worse than any they have thus far experienced. *For* facilities that were built years ago are deteriorating and will have to be completely replaced in the not-too-distant future.

But *for* is a bit formal and won't do for long, complex statements about causes. There are a variety of other introductions, but four of them end in prepositions that force us to use muddy nominalizations rather than specific verbs. Don't begin a sentence with *this was caused by/resulted from/was owing to/was due to:*

> Many of our older cities are facing fiscal crises far worse than any they have thus far experienced. *This is due **to** the deterioration and need for replacement* of facilities that. . . .

Instead, introduce the sentence with *this happened/resulted because* or *we do this because.* You can then state that cause in a full clause, with its own subject-agent and verb-action:

> . . . crises that are far worse than any they have thus far experienced. *This has happened because facilities that were built years ago are deteriorating and will need to be replaced* in the not-too-distant future.

3. Pruning *who/which/that*-clauses. • Sometimes we can edit a string of relative clauses into something more compact simply by changing the clauses a bit. For example:

> Organized labor has lost a good deal of the political power *that* it once used to elect candidates *who* would support programs *that* would benefit rank-and-file workers.

The day is not far off *when* we will all be assigned numbers *that* will identify us and let the government monitor every area of our lives *that* it is interested in controlling.

In sentences such as these, try dropping the *who/which/that* if it's an object.

Organized labor has lost a good deal of the political power _____ it once used to elect candidates *who* would support programs *that* would benefit rank-and-file workers.

The day is not far off *when* we will all be assigned numbers *that* will identify us and let the government monitor every area of our lives _____ it is interested in controlling.

If the *who/which/that* is the *subject* of a clause, you can still drop it, but you will have to rewrite a bit. If the *who/which/that* is the subject of the verb *be,* you have to drop the *be* along with the *who/which/that.*

Any assignments *that are* not yet completed will have to be submitted at a time *that will be* designated by the person *who is* responsible for scheduling.

Any assignments _____ not yet completed will have to be submitted at a time _____ designated by the person _____ responsible for scheduling.

In other cases, you may have to change the verb, too.

Organized labor has lost a good deal of the political power _____ it once used to elect candidates *who would support* programs *that would benefit* rank-and-file workers.

Organized labor has lost a good deal of the political power _____ it once used to elect candidates *who would support* programs _____ benefit*ting* rank-and-file workers.

The day is not far off when we will all be assigned numbers *that* will identify us and let the government monitor every area of our lives _____ it is interested in controlling.

The day is not far off when we will all be assigned numbers _____ identify*ing* us and let*ting* the government monitor every area of our lives _____ it is interested in controlling.

Exercise 4-I

All these sentences are too long. Split them into smaller units; then edit them in the ways we've been discussing.

1. Several activities have already evolved at this college in response to the problems identified in the self-study to meet the ever-expanding range of student learning desires, styles, and capabilities, and these new programs also relate to the traditional goals of the college, which include education of the whole person in the basic skills of liberal education.

2. Two themes that are not separated in their discussion are: first, the apprenticeship nature of graduate medical training, which is therefore at base not a formal process, and, second, teaching competence in the three areas of professional learning, including knowledge, technique, and behavioral skills and attitudes, which require that graduate medical training not exclude formal instruction and work in classroom contexts.

3. Regardless of the fact that it is true that the training program has a long financial problem history and management staff dispute record as a result of unclear organizational responsibility definition, it is equally true that in the period of the last few years or so, it has with considerable success placed in the area of 50 percent of its trainees in various different jobs and positions equal to their training and skill-level preparation.

4. Being alone and being lonely are not the same feeling which a person has resulting from how well that person can draw on resources that he or she has developed during the time he or she was growing into adulthood, which is the period in our lives when we all have to face up to who we are and whether we can live with ourselves for the rest of our lives.

5. As a result of the fact that soaring energy costs have especially placed a burden on those who can least afford the added expense of the energy they use every day—the sick, the older people, and others whose income does not change—and who can least endure the difficult hardship of

lower temperatures, we must create and implement a program of action that would identify those various individuals who can least afford to set their temperatures at a lower level and then provide subsidy support for their oil or gas or coal fuel supply costs.

6. Many city dwellers find it a necessity to give up on life as it exists in the city at the present time as a consequence of things such as dirt and crime that finally defeat them despite the fact that on the occasion of their leaving for more rural environs, they often come to the realization that they wish they again had the intensity and excitement that makes life in the city such a stimulating experience.

7. Nothing offers a test and a challenge of our basic belief in the principle of free speech in a more severe way than the Nazi party of America, which deliberately holds marches and rallies in Jewish communities to enrage those various citizens that experienced the most pain and suffering and misery from German naziism, so that they will arouse violent reactions which will simply give them more publicity that will attract additional members and more money than before.

8. An institution or organization that is disappearing from the general business life in this country is what is known as the men-only club, that seems to have traditionally provided a place or location where business deals and arrangements could be brought to a conclusion in an atmosphere of an intimately male character, for the reason that increasing numbers of women have no reluctance about exercising and using a business power and might that once was in the possession only of men and so require and even go as far as to what could only be called demand the same amenities and conveniences that once were the privilege of men alone.

9. The underlying basic assumption of this procedure assumes: a large enough sample size sufficient so that it does not result in the exclusion of a range of variation that we would not be surprised to find in the total population involved, an analysis not in contradiction with accepted statistical methodological procedures, and a replication of

the study under conditions which have no significant differences from those that existed in other studies of this kind.

10. Lear experiences a failure in the ability to recognize the faithlessness of Goneril and Regan and the honesty of Cordelia and the Fool and also has the inability as to the recognition of who the disguised Kent is, who through a kind of flattery that is not entirely unlike that of Lear's faithless daughters creates in Lear the belief that he "serv'sts" him, for despite the fact that Kent's intentions are of an honorable kind, his flattery of Lear as being someone who would be his "master" is a kind of deceit situation which takes advantage of the unreasonable vanity of Lear, and even gives encouragement to it.

SUMMING UP: CONTROLLING SPRAWL

Here's a checklist for cutting down excessively long sentences.

1. Your sentence is a single punctuated sentence composed of two or more grammatical sentences: Change commas and semicolons to periods:

   In the 1950s, several researchers mapped areas of the brain by stimulating various cortical points with small electrical *charges; the subjects reported* verbally the sensations they experienced as different lobes of the brain were explored.

   . . . with small *electrical charges. The subjects* reported. . . .

(If you've used a colon to introduce a full grammatical sentence instead of a coordinating conjunction or a semicolon, capitalize the first word that follows the colon: The capital letter signals the reader that he can begin processing a completely new sentence.)

2. Your sentence contains two or more long coordinate verb phrases after the subject. Put a period after the first verb phrase; then repeat the subject to change the second verb phrase into an independent sentence:

We first postulated cost-benefit curves for the changeover extending through 1985, taking into consideration the anticipated rate of inflation through *that time, and then projected* a profit ratio to determine whether the investment risk justified our allocating 75 percent of our research efforts in this area.

. . . the anticipated rate of inflation through *that time. We then projected* a profit ratio to determine whether. . . .

3. Your sentence contains a long relative clause beginning with a *which* that refers to the entire preceding sentence: Replace the *which* with a *this* + noun:

Increasing numbers of undergraduates are looking to the master's degree in business administration as their passport to financial success and a world of challenge and *excitement, which reveals* how much students have changed from the more politically and socially aware years of the '60s.

. . . challenge and *excitement. This new interest reveals* how much students have changed from the more politically. . . .

4. Your sentence contains a long relative clause: Rewrite the relative clause as an independent sentence:

If those of lower socioeconomic origins decline to participate in the studies and if their economic status is related to the effectiveness of the treatments, then the study will not effectively evaluate the therapy for the *nonparticipating group, which as a result may undergo* a therapy that is not appropriate to their special medical needs.

. . . will not effectively evaluate the therapy for the *nonparticipating group. As a result, this group may undergo* a therapy that is not. . . .

5. Your sentence has a long adverbial clause beginning with *because, if, although, when, since, while,* etc.: Delete the adverbial conjunction and introduce an appropriate sentence connector:

Although in Elizabethan England the rate of inflation was higher than it ever had been or would ever be again for another three *centuries, peasants* were less affected by it than we might *expect because* many of them grew their own food, made their own clothing, and relied less on the exchange of coin than on the exchange of kind.

In Elizabethan England the rate of inflation was higher than it ever had been or would ever be again for another three *centuries. But peasants* were less affected by it than we might *expect: Many of* them grew their own food, made their own clothing, and relied less on the exchange of coin than on the exchange of kind.

(Note that we also substituted a colon for a *because*.)

6. Your sentence has a colon in the middle of a phrase, introducing a long phrase. Change what follows the colon into an independent clause and a separate sentence:

This procedure necessarily *assumes: that the sample size* is large enough to include the range of variation we would expect to find in the total population and that the analysis of the data is done according to accepted statistical methodology.

This procedure necessarily *assumes the following: (1) The sample size* is large enough to include the range of variation we would expect to find in the total population; (2) the analysis of the data is done according to accepted statistical methodology.

Sustaining the Longer Sentence

Sentences in their variety run from simplicity to complexity, a progression not necessarily reflected in length: a long sentence may be extremely simple in construction—indeed must *be simple if it is to convey its sense easily.*

Sir Herbert Read

A long complicated sentence should force itself upon you, make you know yourself knowing it . . . .

Gertrude Stein

All length is torture . . . .

William Shakespeare, *Antony and Cleopatra*, 4.12

The ability to write clear, crisp sentences* that never go beyond twenty words is a considerable achievement. You'll never confuse your reader with sprawl, wordiness, or muddy abstraction. But if you never write a sentence longer than twenty words, you'll be like a pianist who uses only the middle octave: You can play the tune, but not with much richness or variation.

Every competent writer has to know how to write a concise sentence and how to edit a long one down to comprehensible length. But a writer also has to know how to manage a long sentence gracefully, how to make it as clear and as vigorous as a series of short ones.

Now, several long clauses* in a single grammatical sentence* do not in themselves constitute formless sprawl. Here is a sentence with eighteen subordinate clauses, seventeen of them leading up to a single main clause* and the eighteenth bringing up the end:

> Now if nature should intermit her course and leave altogether, though it were but for a while, the observation of her own laws; if those principal and mother elements of the world, whereof all things in this lower world are made, should loose the qualities which now they have; if the frame of that heavenly arch erected over our heads should loosen and dissolve itself; if celestial spheres should forget their wonted motions, and by irregular volubility turn themselves any way as it might happen; if the prince of the lights of heaven, which now as a giant doth run his unwearied course, should, as it were through a languishing faintness, begin to stand and to rest himself; if the moon should wander from her beaten way, the times and seasons of the year blend themselves by disordered and confused mixture, the winds breathe out their last gasp, the clouds yield no rain, the earth be defeated of heavenly influence, the fruits of the earth pine away as children at the withered breasts of their mother no longer able to yield them relief;—what would become of man himself, whom these things now do all serve?
>
> —Thomas Hooker, *Of the Laws of Ecclesiastical Polity*, 1594

Whatever else we may want to say about that sentence, it does not sprawl. Its sixteenth-century elaboration builds beyond what our modern ear is comfortable with, but stylistically, its clauses fit together as neatly as the universe Hooker describes. So it is not length alone or number of clauses alone that we ought to worry about, but rather sentences without shape or rhythm.

There are a few simple ways you can extend the line of a sentence beyond a common measure and still be graceful and clear. The most frequent, perhaps the most elegant, is coordination*.

COORDINATION

We can join grammatically equal segments with *and, but, yet,* or *or* anywhere in a sentence. But we do it most gracefully after the subject*, in the predicate*. If we create a long subject, our reader has to hold his breath until he gets to a verb*:

Public service advertising that trumpets corporate altruism

and

commercial advertising that tries to increase sales

} sometimes serve conflicting interests.

An advertisement that urges us to buy an outdoor barbecue fueled by natural gas

and

another that tells us to conserve energy by turning down our thermostats to 68°,

} for example, cannot be easily reconciled.

If we compare these examples with the next ones, we see how a sentence with a shorter subject and a longer predicate* can move along with a bit more grace:

Sometimes, we can sense a conflict of interest between

{ public service advertising that trumpets corporate altruism

and

commercial advertising that tries to increase sales.

For example, it's difficult to reconcile

{ an advertisement that urges us to buy an outdoor barbecue fueled by natural gas

and

another that tells us to conserve energy by turning down our thermostats to 68°.

In general, a vigorous sentence moves quickly from a short and concrete subject through a strong verb to its complement*, where we can more gracefully elaborate our syntax and more fully develop our ideas. So if we extend a sentence by deliberately coordinating parts of it, we should coordinate after the subject more often than before the verb.

Problems with Coordination

If we use coordination to build gracefully longer sentences, we have to be careful to avoid two problems.

1. *Faulty Parallelism.* • When we coordinate sentence parts that have different grammatical structures, we may create an offensively nonparallel sentence. A common rule of rhetoric and grammar is that we can coordinate members only of the same grammatical structure: clause and clause, predicate and predicate, prepositional phrase* and prepositional phrase. Most careful writers would avoid this:

These advertisements persuade us

that the corporation supports environmentalism

but not

to buy its frivolous products.

Corrected:

... persuade us $\left\{ \begin{array}{l} \textit{that the corporation supports} \\ \text{environmentalism} \\ \qquad \text{but not} \\ \textit{that we should buy} \text{ its frivolous} \\ \text{products.} \end{array} \right.$

This also would be considered nonparallel:

The committee recommends $\left\{ \begin{array}{l} \textit{completely revising the curriculum} \text{ in} \\ \text{applied education in order to reflect} \\ \text{new trends in local employment} \\ \qquad\qquad \text{and} \end{array} \right.$

$\left\{\begin{array}{l}\textit{that the administrative}\\ \textit{structure} \text{ of the division}\\ \text{be modified to reflect}\\ \text{the new curriculum}\end{array}\right.$

Corrected:

. . . recommends $\left\{\begin{array}{l}\textit{that the curriculum} \text{ in applied}\\ \text{education be completely revised in}\\ \text{order to reflect new trends in local}\\ \text{employment}\\ \qquad\text{and}\\ \textit{that the administrative structure} \text{ of the}\\ \text{division be modified to reflect the}\\ \text{new curriculum.}\end{array}\right.$

And yet some nonparallel coordinations occur fairly often in well-written prose. Writers frequently join a noun* phrase with a *how*-clause:

Every attempt will be made to delineate $\left\{\begin{array}{l}\textit{the problems} \text{ of biomedical education}\\ \text{among the underdeveloped nations}\\ \qquad\text{and}\\ \textit{how a coordinated effort can address}\\ \text{them in the most economical and}\\ \text{expeditious way.}\end{array}\right.$

Or an adjective* or adverb* with a prepositional phrase:

The grant proposal appears to have been written $\left\{\begin{array}{l}\textit{intelligently,}\\ \textit{carefully,}\\ \\ \qquad\text{and}\\ \\ \textit{with the full cooperation} \text{ of all the}\\ \text{agencies whose interests this project}\\ \text{involves.}\end{array}\right.$

Some teachers and editors would insist on rewriting these into parallel form:

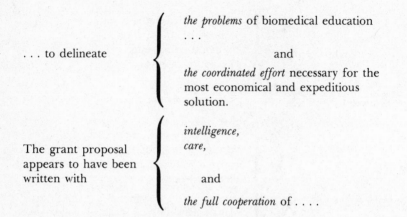

But most educated readers don't even notice the "faulty" parallelism here, much less find it offensive.

2. *Lost Connections.* • What will bother readers more than mildly faulty parallelism is a grammatical coordination so long that they either lose track of its internal connections or, worse, mistake those connections:

> Every teacher ought to remind himself daily that his students are vulnerable people, insecure and uncertain about those everyday, ego-bruising moments that adults no longer concern themselves with, and that they do not understand that one day they will become as confident and as secure as the adults that bruise them.

That momentary flicker of hesitation about where to connect

> and that they do not understand that one day they

is enough to interrupt the flow of the sentence.

If you can't bring the second coordinate member closer than ten or twelve words to where it connects, try repeating a key word that connects them.

> Every teacher ought to remind himself daily that his students are vulnerable people, insecure and uncertain about those everyday, ego-bruising moments that adults have learned to cope with, *to remind himself* that his students do not understand that one day they will become as confident and as secure as the adults that bruise them.

And, of course, you can always begin a new sentence:

> . . . adults no longer concern themselves with. Teachers should remind themselves that their students do not understand . . . .

EXTENDING THE SENTENCE

Resumptive Modifiers

A device that shares one characteristic of coordination but creates a somewhat different effect is a pattern we will call a *resumptive modifier**. With a resumptive modifier, you repeat a key noun, verb, or adjective and then *resume* the line of thought, elaborating on what went before. The effect is to let the reader pause for a moment, then move on. Compare:

> For several years the Columbia Broadcasting System created and developed situation comedies that were the best that American TV had to offer such as "The Mary Tyler Moore Show" and "All in the Family" that sparkled with wit and invention.

> For several years, the Columbia Broadcasting System created and developed situation *comedies* that were the best that American TV had to offer,
> > *comedies* such as "The Mary Tyler Moore Show" and "All in the Family,"
> > *comedies* that sparkled with wit and invention.

That first sentence verges on rhythmic monotony at best, and at worst collapses into sprawl. The writer tacked on a relative clause*, *comedies **that** were the best,* and then without a pause a second, *"the Family" **that** sparkled with wit and invention.* The resumptive modifier in the second example lets us pause for a moment, catch our breath, and then move on. It also helps resolve any problems we might have with an ambiguous modifier, and provides one more point in the sentence where we can create a touch of emphasis. If you pick your spots carefully—and not too frequently—you can use this device to highlight important words.

You can pause and resume with parts of speech other than nouns. Here with adjectives:

> It was American writers who first used a vernacular that was both *true* and *lyrical*,
> > *true* to the rhythms of the working man and *lyrical* in its celebration of the land.

Here with verbs:

> Man has been defined by some as the only animal that can *laugh* at grief,
> > *laugh* at the pain and tragedy that defines his fate.

Summative Modifiers

Somewhat similar is the *summative modifier*.* With a summative modifier, you end a segment of a sentence with a comma, sum up in a noun or noun phrase* what you have just said, and then continue with a relative clause. Compare these:

> In the last five years, our population growth has dropped to almost zero, *which* in years to come will have profound social implications.

> In the last five years, our population growth has dropped to almost zero,
> > *a demographic event that* in years to come will have profound social implications.

> Scientists have finally unraveled the mysteries of the human gene, *which* may lead to the control of such dread diseases as cancer and birth defects.

> Scientists have finally unraveled the mysteries of the human gene,
> > *a discovery that* may lead to the control of such dread diseases as cancer and birth defects.

The summative modifier avoids the gracelessness and the potential ambiguity of a vague *which* and lets the writer extend the line of the sentence without becoming monotonous.

Free Modifiers

A third kind of modifier that lets you continue the line of a sentence but still avoid monotony resembles the previous two but functions a bit differently. It follows the verb but comments on the subject. It usually makes more specific what you assert in the preceding clause. Compare:

> However violent King Kong appeared, he always had a hint of the noble savage about him who protected his fair captive against prehistoric monsters and who treated her with the gentleness of an exceptionally hairy and overgrown but basically decent Tarzan.

> However violent King Kong appeared, he always had a hint of the noble savage about him,
> > *protecting* his fair captive against prehistoric monsters, *treating* her with the gentleness of an exceptionally hairy and overgrown but basically decent Tarzan.

As in this example, these modifiers most often begin with an *-ing* form of a verb:

> The Scopes monkey trial was a watershed in American religious thinking,
> > *legitimizing* the contemporary interpretation of the Bible and *making* literal fundamentalism a backwater of antiintellectual theology.

But they can also begin with a past participle*:

> Leonardo da Vinci was a man of powerful intellect,
> > *driven* by an insatiable curiosity and *haunted* by a vision of artistic expression.

And with adjectives:

> In 1939, the United States began to assist the British in their struggle against Germany,
> > *fully aware* that it was involving itself in another world war.

Because these modifying phrases attach to their sentences more loosely than resumptive or summative modifiers, we'll call them *free modifiers**.

Exercise 5-I

In these next sentences, create resumptive, summative, and free modifiers. The first five have a word in italics to use as the start of the resumptive modifier and a word in parentheses at the end to use as the start of the resumptive modifier. Then pick four or five sentences and create a free modifier on your own. For example:

> Within ten years, we could meet 25 percent of our energy needs with solar *energy*. (a possibility)

Resumptive:

> Within ten years, we could meet 25 percent of our energy needs with solar *energy, energy* that is safe, cheap and plentiful.

Summative:

> Within ten years, we could meet 25 percent of our energy needs with solar energy, *a possibility* that no one could have anticipated just ten years ago.

Free:

> Within ten years, we could meet 25 percent of our energy needs with solar energy, freeing ourselves of dependence on OPEC oil.

(Many of these sentences can also be edited for redundancy, wordiness, heavy nominalizations, etc.)

1. Many different school systems are making a return back to old-fashioned traditional education in the *basics*. (a change)
2. Within the period of the next few years or so, automobile manufacturers will not be able to avoid meeting new and more stringent-type mileage *requirements*. (a challenge)
3. The reasons for why we age is a *matter* that has puzzled and perplexed humanity for millennia. (mystery)

4. The majority of the young people in the modern world of today cannot even begin to achieve an understanding or grasp of the *insecurity* that a large number of older people had experience of during the period known as the Great Depression. (a failure)
5. The recent successful accomplishment of test-tube fertilization of embryos has raised many *issues* of an ethical nature that are troubling both scientists and laypeople. (an event)
6. Many people who lived during the Victorian era were appalled when Darwin put forth the suggestion that their ancestry may have included apes.
7. In 1961, the U.S. government made the announcement that it would put the first man on the moon.
8. Nikita Khrushchev once advanced the claim that by 1975 communism would bury the system of capitalism.
9. In the 1960s the Supreme Court passed the rule that anyone under arrest for a crime that he or she may or may not have committed had to be given the widest possible benefit of legal doubt.
10. American prisons are for the most part schools for crime and pits of degradation.

In these next, prune the redundancy and the abstraction and create coordinate modifiers of your own devising. For example, here is a coordinate resumptive modifier built on to number 5 above:

> . . . ethical *issues* that are troubling both scientists and laymen, *issues* that yield easily to *neither historical religious principles nor contemporary legal theory.*

11. The general concept of systematic skepticism is in effect a kind of denial that there can ever be any kind of certain knowledge of reality screened and influenced by human perception.
12. The originating point when the field of scientific inquiry began to develop is to be found for the most part in the individual and personal observations of naive primitive peoples about the natural things that appear to occur in a regular way.

13. In the period known to scholars and historians as the Renaissance period, increases in affluence and stability in the area of political affairs had the practical consequence and outcome of allowing streams of thought of various different kinds of merge and flow together with one another.

14. During the recent period of about the last few years or so, we have been witness to a very large number of various specific acts and deeds that mainly involve terroristic components.

MOVEMENT AND MOMENTUM

There's no reason why a well-managed long sentence shouldn't be as clear and as crisp as several short ones. A writer who can handle a long sentence gracefully lets us take a breath at reasonable intervals and at appropriate places; he probably echoes one part of his sentence against another with coordinated and parallel elements. And if he avoids muddling about in abstraction and weak passives, he invests his sentences with the directness and energy that a readable style demands.

But if a sentence is to flow easily, its writer should also avoid making us hesitate over words and phrases that break its major grammatical links; we should be able to complete all those links quickly and surely. Here, for example, is a sentence that does not flow:

> China, in order to exert in a more direct way its influence among the Eastern Bloc nations, in 1958 began in a carefully orchestrated manner a diplomatic offensive against the Soviet Union.

This flows more smoothly:

> In 1958, in order to exert a more direct influence among the Eastern Bloc nations, China began a carefully orchestrated diplomatic offensive against the Soviet Union.

Both sentences make us pause, but the first forces us to hold our breath after the subject, *China,* as we wait for the verb, *began;* the second lets us take a breath halfway through, when we finish the second introductory phrase, and then lets us quickly connect the subject with its verb. The only change in the two versions is the order of the phrases. In the first sentence, the important grammatical connections are broken; in the second, they are intact. And in the first, the phrases are ordered from longer to shorter; in the second, from shorter to longer.

Grammatical Connections

Normal English word order is subject-verb-object*. All things being equal, we should avoid breaking the connections between those sentence parts. A reader is always looking to complete a major grammatical phrase and to begin processing a new one. The major junctures where a reader can do that are, of course, at the end of the whole sentence and at the end of any of its clauses. But he also wants to "close" the subject with its verb. If you delay or muddy that subject-verb connection, your reader will hesitate, backtrack, reread looking for it. And as a consequence, your reader will feel your style to be tense and uncertain.

Given that principle of "closure," we can explain why the second example sentence reads more easily than the first. In the second, nothing separates the subject from its verb or the verb from its object:

(verb + object)   In order to exert + a more direct influence

(subject + verb)   China + began

(verb + object)   began + a carefully orchestrated diplomatic offensive

But in the first version, the grammatical connections are interrupted:

China [in order to exert . . . Eastern Bloc nations] began

exert [in a more direct way] its influence

began [in a carefully orchestrated manner] a diplomatic offensive

Now it is true that many competent writers do interrupt the subject-verb link with phrases and clauses. And it is true that many short adverbs fit between the subject and verb quite comfortably:

> Scientists the world over *deliberately* write in a style that is aloof, impersonal, and objective.

But longer phrases and clauses fit there less comfortably:

> Scientists the world over, *because they deliberately write in a style that is aloof, impersonal, and objective,* have difficulty communicating with laypeople ignorant of scientific method.

If nothing else precedes the subject, you lose little by moving a long modifying phrase or clause to the beginning of its sentence:

> *Because scientists the world over deliberately write in a style that is aloof, impersonal, and objective,* they have difficulty communicating with laypeople ignorant of scientific method.

Placing your modifier at the beginning of its sentence lets you avoid that flicker of hesitation which, repeated, will eventually retard the flow of a style.

Exercise 5-II

These sentences contain unfortunate interruptions. Correct the interruption and add a summative, resumptive, or loose modifier of your own creation. Also edit to eliminate wordiness.

1. The construction of the Interstate Highway System, owing to the fact that Congress, on the occasion when it originally voted funds for it, did not anticipate the cost of inflation, has run into insoluble problems.
2. Such conduct or behavior, for whatever reasons profferred, is rarely not at least to some degree prejudicial to good order and discipline.
3. TV game shows, due to the fact that they have an appeal to the basic cupidity in us all, are just about the most popular shows that appear on daytime TV.
4. The merit selection of those who serve as judges, given the

low quality and character of elected officials, is an idea whose time came long ago.

5. The field of high-energy physics, working with certain devices that can actually accelerate particles to a speed almost as fast as the speed of light, is exploring the ultimate nature and makeup of matter.

6. The continued and unabated emission of carbon dioxide gas into the atmospheric environment, unless there is a marked reduction prior to the end of the century, will eventually result in a change in the climate of the world as we know it today.

7. Only those individuals who are the rich, in the case that the government in advance of the next congressional election does not make any provisions for all political candidates for office to receive campaign funds, will, in large enough numbers to assure a wide selection of candidates, have the ability for seeking public office.

8. Insistence that there is no proof by scientific means of a certain causal link between the activity of smoking and various disease entities such as cardiac heart failure and malignant cancer conditions, despite the fact that there is a strong statistical correlation between the act of smoking and disease, continues to be the official stated position and policy of the cigaret companies.

9. Medical science, in about the last half century or so, due to the fact of great strides being made in the detection and even anticipation of sicknesses and diseases that in the last half century would simply make an appearance in our midst to result in the terrible devastation of whole populations, now has a year in advance the capability for the early prediction of future outbreaks of disease entities such as influenza.

A FINE POINT: Small Connections

Sometimes, we awkwardly split an adjective from the modifying phrase that follows it: We put the adjective before a noun it modifies, and the phrase that modifies the adjective, after the noun:

The accountant has given *as accurate* **a projection** *as any that could be provided.*

We are facing *a more serious* **decision** *than what you described earlier.*

A *close* **relationship** *to the one just discovered* is the degree to which *similar* **genetic material** *to that of related species* can be modified by *different* **DNA chains** *from the ones first selected.by Adams and Walsh.*

Another **course of action** *than the present one* is necessary to accumulate *sufficient* **capital** *to complete such* **projects** *as those you have described.*

In each case, the adjective—usually an adjective being compared—is split from its following phrase:

as accurate . . . as any that could be provided

more serious . . . than what

close . . . to the one

similar . . . to that

different . . . from the ones

another . . . than the present

sufficient . . . to complete

such . . as those you

We can keep the rhythm moving more surely if we put the adjective after the noun, right next to the phrase that completes the adjective:

The accountant has given **a projection** *as accurate as any that could have been provided.*

We are facing **a decision** *more serious than what you described earlier.*

A relationship *close to the one just discovered* is the degree to which **genetic material** *similar to that of related species* can be modified by **DNA chains** *different from the ones first selected by Adams and Walsh.*

A course of action *other than the present one* is necessary to accumulate **capital** *sufficient to complete* **projects** *such as those you describe.*

Some of the adjectives that we most frequently split off from their modifying phrases are these: *more than, less than, other than, as . . . as, similar to, equal to, identical to, same as, different from, such as, separate from, distant from, related to, close to, next to, difficult to, easy to, necessary to, sufficient to, adequate to.*

Exercise 5-III

Each of the following contains several adjective phrases awkwardly disjoined. Edit the passages to reunite the phrases and to make the style clearer and more direct.

1. The reason why an identical ecological impact statement to that submitted the previous year indicates that it will again be difficult data to evaluate is that there is still no independent verifying information from that which has been supplied by the applicant in our possession.
2. Under circumstances in which similar EKG readings are obtained to those obtained earlier, other conditions than cardiac insufficiency must come under suspicion. The same procedures as those outlined in the previous section must be closely adhered to on the expectation that as effective results as those outlined there are to be achieved in such cases.
3. As a result of the reorganization of the marketing research division, more accurate information than that which has been received in the past should allow the identification of different populations from those that have been traditionally aimed at. This will be relatively easy information to process in analysis as a result of the fact that there has already been accumulated such demographic data as the average financial income, expenditure patterns, etc., for many different markets. As a result of all this, greater efficiency than that which we achieved in our earlier operation last year may be a reasonable expectation.

Short-to-Long Order

This principle of quick, sure connections explains why a sentence with a short subject reads just a bit more easily than a sentence with a long subject:

> *A discovery that will change the course of world history and the very foundations of our understanding of who we are and our place in the scheme of things* is imminent.

The longer you make a reader stay with a subject before you reach its verb, the less smoothly you move him through a sentence. Compare this:

> A *discovery* is imminent that will change the course of world history and the very foundations of our understanding of ourselves and our place in the scheme of things.

In fact, English has several stylistic devices that specifically let us transform long subjects into short ones:

1. *Moveable relative clauses* • In the example you just read, I was able to shorten the subject and lengthen the predicate when I shifted the relative clause away from the subject to a position after the verb. Another example:

> A marketing approach *that will allow us to take advantage of shifting demographic patterns and changing tastes* has been developed.

> A marketing approach has been developed *that will allow us to take advantage of shifting demographic patterns and changing tastes.*

Don't shift the clause if it results in an ambiguous construction. In this next one, the shifted clause seems to modify *staff:*

> A marketing approach has been developed by the **staff** *that will allow us to take advantage of shifting demographic patterns and changing tastes.*

2. *Passives* again* • The passive is another device that we can use to exchange a long subject for a short one.

> During the first years of our Republic, *a series of brilliant and virtuous presidents committed to a democracy yet confident in their own special competence* conducted **its administration.**

> During the first years of our Republic, **its administration** was conducted by *a series of brilliant and virtuous presidents committed to a democracy yet confident in their own special competence.*

> *Astronomers, physicists, and a host of other researchers entirely familiar with the problems raised by quasars* have confirmed **these observations.**

These observations have been confirmed by *astronomers, physicists, and a host of other researchers entirely familiar with the problems raised by quasars.*

3. *It*-shift • This allows us to shift a long introductory clause to a position after the verb:

That domestic oil prices must eventually rise to the level set by OPEC in order to force oil conservation is inevitable.

It is inevitable *that domestic oil prices must eventually rise to the level set by OPEC in order to force oil conservation.*

Some editors object to this anticipatory expletive *it* because they believe, mistakenly, that the *it* is a vague pronoun. In a passage with several other *its,* this expletive *it* might be confusing:

While *it* is true that *it* now requires more energy to produce methanol alcohol than *it* provides, *it* might well prove to be a cost-saving additive to fuel if *it* can be proved that *its* cost can be lowered substantially.

4. *What*-shift • When the long subject phrase refers to something other than a person, you can push that subject toward the end of its sentence with a *what*-shift:

The difficulty of reconciling traditional Christian doctrine regarding family life with the realities of late twentieth-century social forces constitutes the single greatest threat to American Catholicism.

What constitutes the single greatest threat to American Catholicism **is** *the difficulty of reconciling traditional Christian doctrine regarding family life with the realities of late twentieth-century social forces.*

(This is also an important device to focus a reader's attention on a particular topic, as we shall see in the next lesson.)

5. *Subject-complement* switching* • Sometimes, we can simply switch the subject and complement, especially around the linking verb *be:*

The source of the American attitude toward rural dialects is **more interesting.**

More interesting is *the source of the American attitude toward rural dialects.*

We can make a similar switch with other verbs:

The failure of the administrators to halt the continually rising costs of hospital care lies **at the heart of the problem.**

At the heart of the problem lies *the failure of the administration to halt the continually rising costs of hospital care.*

An Exception to a Rule • We've just seen one set of exceptions to a rule: In the passive and in the sentences we just read, we've reversed subjects and complements so that the agent of an action does not appear at the beginning of its clause. The principle of short-to-long order sometimes leads us to set aside another rule: keeping grammatical connections tight. Consider this sentence:

No one can explain why that first primeval superatom exploded and thereby created the universe *in a few words.*

The object of *explain,* the clause *why that first primeval superatom exploded and thereby created the universe,* is much longer than the short modifier of *explain, in a few simple words.* We can create a smoother line if we put that shorter, less important phrase before the longer, more important object, even if it means separating the object from its verb. (And in the bargain, we make it clearer what that modifier modifies.)

No one can explain *in a few words* why that first primeval superatom exploded and thereby created the universe.

SOME PROBLEMS WITH MODIFIERS

Sentences can grow both long and confusing when we add lots of modifiers. And because the logical and grammatical connections between the modifier and the thing modified sometimes become unclear or ambiguous, we also risk misleading our readers.

Dangling Modifiers

A modifier "dangles" when its implied subject differs from the specific subject of the clause that follows it:

> In order to limit the spread of the infection, the entire area was sealed off.

(The implied subject of *limit,* some person, is different from the subject of the main clause, *the entire area.*)

> Resuming negotiations after a break of several days, the same issues confronted both the union and the company.

(The implied subject of *resuming, the union and the company,* is different from the subject of the main clause, *the same issues.*)

Constructions like these rarely interfere with clear communication. But since they cause some readers to hesitate for a moment, you ought to avoid them on general principles. Either rewrite the introductory phrase so that it has its own subject or make the subject of the main clause agree with the implied subject of the introductory phrase:

> In order for us to limit the spread of the infection, the entire area was sealed off.

> In order to limit the spread of the infection, the police sealed off the entire area.

> When *the union and the company* resumed negotiations, the same issues confronted them.

> Resuming negotiations after a break of several days, *the union and the company* confronted the same issues.

Some modifiers that seem to dangle are in fact acceptable. If either the modifier or the subject of the main clause is part of the metadiscourse*, the modifier will seem entirely appropriate to most readers:

In order to start the motor, **it is essential** that the retroflex cam connecting rod be disengaged.

To summarize, *unemployment* in the southern tier of counties remains the state's major economic and social problem.

Misplaced Modifiers

A second problem with modifiers is that sometimes they seem to modify two things, or the wrong thing. One kind of ambiguous modifier can refer either forward or back:

Overextending oneself in strenuous physical activity *too frequently* results in a variety of physical ailments.

We failed *entirely* to understand the complexities of the problem.

In each of these, the modifier can just as easily appear in an unambiguous position:

Overextending oneself *too frequently* in strenuous exercise . . . .

Overextending oneself in physical exercise results *too frequently* in a variety of physical ailments.

We *entirely* failed to understand . . . .

We failed to understand *entirely* . . . .

A second kind of ambiguity occurs when a modifier at the end of a clause or sentence can modify either a neighboring or a more distant phrase:

Scientists have learned that their observations are as necessarily subjective as those in any other field *in recent years.*

We can move the modifier to a less ambiguous position:

In recent years, scientists have learned that . . . .

Scientists have learned that *in recent years,* their observations . . . .

In these cases, we can also use a resumptive modifier to make clear what a modifier is supposed to modify. In the next sentence, for example, what is it that dictates—the contingencies, the components, or the process?

> It may be that there are contingencies among the components of the process that would dictate one order rather than another.

A moment's thought suggests that the contingencies dictate, but why should we cause our reader to pause even for a moment to understand how one idea connects to another? The sentence should make it clear. A resumptive modifier would help:

> It may be that there are contingencies among the components of the process, *contingencies* that would dictate one order rather than another.

Pronoun reference. A long sentence can also create problems with pronoun reference. If there is the slightest chance that a pronoun will confuse your reader, don't hesitate to repeat a word. And if you can conveniently make one set of your nouns plural and another singular, you can use those different singular and plural pronouns to distinguish what you're referring to. Compare these:

> *Physicians* must never forget that *their patients* are vitally concerned about *their* treatment and *their* prognosis, but that *they* often are unwilling to ask for fear of what *they* will say.

> A *physician* must never forget that *his patients* are vitally concerned about *their* treatment and *their* prognosis, but that *they* are often unwilling to ask for fear of what *he* will say.

(We'll take up the matter of the masculine *he* in Lesson 9.)

Exercise 5-IV

Rearrange the elements in these sentences so that the sentences flow from shorter elements to longer ones.

1. The new barbarians display a response to intense aesthetic experience that takes the form of "Wow" usually, so far as their range of expressiveness is concerned.

2. I will now sketch the solar system as it was conceived by pre-Copernican astronomers ordinarily in simple outline for you.

3. Historians impose not just their private view of historical relevancy but the implied view of their whole social matrix on the past with little sense of scholarly bias.

4. We can perhaps if we study the psychoanalytic theories that Freud created for his scholarly and therefore largely male audience honestly and objectively in all their masculine assumptions understand why psychiatry has assigned the major source of a man's mental disorder to his mother so often.

5. The isolation of various clotting mechanisms in higher mammals is the next point.

6. The relation of individual objective bits of data to general principles applicable at all times and everywhere is a more important defining feature of the modern mind.

7. That Woodrow Wilson's refusal to take the leadership of the United States Senate into his confidence caused the defeat of the Versailles Treaty is universally acknowledged.

8. Two historically antagonistic chambers, a variety of hereditary and appointed senators whose responsibility in administrative affairs is relatively slight making up one and an elective body that carries on the important legislative activities making up the other, constitute the legislative branch.

9. A virus which bears no known relation to any other form of protein-based life was discovered last year, though, in England.

10. That the need to monitor the flow of hard currency across national boundaries more carefully in the years to come is an equally pressing matter is just as important, in the opinion of most international monetary experts.

These sentences suffer from a variety of dangling, misplaced, ambiguous, and otherwise badly constructed or positioned modifiers. Correct them, and then edit the sentences in any other way you see fit.

11. Having no previous familiarity with the mechanism, metal

deposit detection efforts by means of its use were met with a lack of success.

12. With every expectation of success, new efforts to resolve the differences that have resulted in interference with communication in a short time should be initiated.

13. Realizing that the undergraduate curriculum must be completely reevaluated in the next few weeks, proposals have suddenly appeared on the agenda that had received earlier discussion.

14. After making an audit of all internal operations in the summer of 1978 a second audit examined the record of foreign affiliates that had not been previously audited by their local headquarters.

SUMMING UP: CONTROLLING LONG SENTENCES

1. Avoid writing long, rhythmically unbroken sentences consisting of one clause tacked on to another tacked on to another tacked on to another.

2. To create a gracefully long sentence, use one or more of the following devices:

a. Coordination

Besides the fact that no previous civilization has experienced such rapid alterations in the condition of daily life, the life of the mind has changed greatly too.

No previous civilization has experienced such rapid alterations *in the condition of daily life* or *in the life of the mind*.

b. Resumptive modifiers

Our discovery that the earth was not at the center of the universe reshaped our understanding not only of where we are but of who we are, which was changed again by Darwin, and again by Freud, and again by Einstein.

Our discovery that the earth was not at the center of the universe reshaped our *understanding* not only of where we are but of who we are, *an understanding* that was changed again by Darwin, and again by Freud, and again by Einstein.

c. Summative modifiers

Most business people and government officials have maintained that the only way out of our current energy crisis is to construct a massive synthetic fuel industry, which is rejected by those environmentalists who argue that we can achieve the same net result by equally massive investments in mass transportation and insulation.

Most business people and government officials have maintained that the only way out of our current energy crisis is to construct a massive synthetic fuel industry, *a position* rejected by those environmentalists who argue that we can achieve the same net result by equally massive investments in mass transportation and insulation.

d. Free modifiers

The Dog Whelk is one of the most common snails found in the intertidal zone of the northern East Coast which proliferates in especially dense colonies on rocky shelves from Maine all the way to the Arctic Circle.

The Dog Whelk is one of the most common snails found in the intertidal zone of the northern East Coast, *proliferating* in especially dense colonies on rocky shelves from Maine all the way to the Arctic Circle.

3. To keep up the momentum in a long sentence, aim for the following:

a. Fairly short elements before the verb, longer ones after it:

*The germ of a mathematical truth that eventually led to the invention of the Calculus **lies** behind Zeno's Paradox.*

*Behind Zeno's Paradox **lies** the germ of a mathematical truth that eventually led to the invention of the Calculus.*

b. Uninterrupted links between subject-verb and verb-object:

The Protagoras, *despite its questionable logic and rather superficial philosophical content,* **remains** one of Plato's most dramatically appealing dialogues.

Despite its questionable logic and rather superficial philosophical content,

the Protagoras remains one of Plato's most dramatically appealing dialogues.

On the other hand, if the object is very long and the interrupting phrase is very short, put the modifier between the verb and object.

Few politicians are willing to acknowledge that the bulk of the electorate regards them essentially as parasites *even to themselves.*

Few politicians are willing to acknowledge *even to themselves* that the bulk of the electorate regards them essentially as parasites.

Lesson Six

Sentences in Context

The two capital secrets in the art of prose composition are these: first the philosophy of transition and connection; or the art by which one step in an evolution of thought is made to arise out of another: all fluent and effective composition depends on the connections; secondly, the way in which sentences are made to modify each other; for the most powerful effects in written eloquence arise out of this reverberation, as it were, from each other in a rapid succession of sentences.

Thomas de Quincey

Good beginning maketh a good ending.

Anonymous

All's well that ends well.

William Shakespeare

So far, we've talked about clear and direct writing as if we wrote only individual sentences*, independent of any larger context or governing intention. And it's true that in individual sentences we can achieve a kind of singular clarity. But if those individually clear sentences don't emphasize our most important ideas, if those sentences don't fit the context of the sentences around them, then no matter how clear those individual sentences are, they won't constitute a cohesive discourse.

CONTEXTS

One of the facts that make English such a rich and complex language is that our optimally clear and direct order of

subject*	verb*	object*
agent*	action*	goal*

may not be the best order if we want to be emphatic and cohesive. For example, few principles of style are more widely repeated than the one that says don't use the indirect passive* but rather the direct and vigorous active.* Not

> A black hole *is created by* the collapse of a dead star into a point perhaps no larger than a marble.

but

> The collapse of a dead star into a point perhaps no larger than a marble *creates* a black hole.

But suppose the context for either of those sentences was this:

> Some astonishing questions about the nature of the universe have been raised by scientists exploring the nature of black holes in space.[_____] So much matter compressed into so little volume changes the fabric of the space around it in profoundly astonishing ways.

By this time, our sense of coherence and rhythm should tell us that this context calls for the passive, not the active. And the reasons are not far to seek: The last part of the first sentence, *the nature of black holes in space,* introduces what would be the object of an active verb in the second sentence:

> . . . collapse creates *a black hole.*

But we can improve the transition between the first and second sentences by shifting that object to the beginning of its sentence, closer to the end of the sentence that comes before. We can make it the subject of a passive* verb:

> . . . the nature of *black holes in space. A black hole* is created. . . .

The problem—and the challenge—of English prose is that in almost every sentence we write, we have to strike the best compromise among the emphasis we want to achieve, the principles of coherence and cohesion that fuse separate sentences into a whole discourse, those principles of clarity and directness that we discussed earlier, and what the grammar of English lets us create. But in that compromise, we always give priority to emphasis and cohesion, to what makes a discourse whole and cohesive.

There are two complementary principles of order and emphasis. We've just mentioned one of them:

> Whenever possible, express at the beginning of a sentence ideas already stated, referred to, implied, safely assumed, familiar—whatever we might call old, repeated, relatively predictable, less important, readily accessible information, especially metadiscourse*.

The other principle is this:

> Express at the end of a sentence the least predictable, the least accessible, the newest, the most significant and striking information.

The logical consequence of these two is this:

> The beginning of a sentence should orient a reader toward new information, should provide a context for him to move from the known to the unknown, from the predictable to the unpredictable.

In every sentence, we should do more than express agencies and actions clearly: By how we arrange the flow of our ideas, we should also communicate what is less important, and what is more.

ENDING STRONG

As a general rule, manage your sentences so that you express your most striking ideas at the end. In fact, this end position is so important that we could use a term to name it. When you utter a sentence, your voice rises and falls. When you approach a major break in the flow of words, particularly at the end of a sentence, you ordinarily raise your pitch and stress on one of those last words just a bit more strongly than on the others:

> *. . . a bit more strongly than on the* ^{o}
> $thers.$

Natural rhythm, pitch, and stress signal the end of a sentence more prominently than they signal its beginning. Let's call that part of a sentence given the strongest stress, the *stress* of the sentence. The stress can be on just the last word, or on the last few words, depending on how much new information we're expressing.

You can manage the information in this stressed part of the sentence in a number of ways. You can, of course, put your newest and most important information there in the first place. Often enough though, even the best writers have to edit their sentences after they've written them to get that information into the right place. One way to edit what we write is to move less important phrases and clauses *away* from the end of a sentence, so that we leave exposed at the end what we want to stress.

> The data that are offered to establish the existence of ESP do not make believers of us *for the most part.*
>
> *For the most part,* the data that are offered to establish the existence of ESP do not make believers of us.

In other cases, we can simply lop off final unnecessary words and phrases until we get to the information we want to stress, leaving that information in the final position:

> Sociobiologists are making the provocative claim that our genes largely determine our social behavior in the way we act in situations we find around us every day.

Since *social behavior* means *the way we act* . . . , we can just drop everything after *behavior:*

> Sociobiologists are making the provocative claim that our genes largely determine our social behavior.

Moving the important information *to* the end of a sentence is another way we can manage the flow of ideas. And the sentence you just read illustrates a missed opportunity to do so. This would have been more cohesive and emphatic:

> Another way we can manage the flow of ideas is by moving the most important information *to* the end of the sentence.

Sentences that introduce a paragraph or a new section of a paper are frequently of an X is Y form. One part announces the new topic; the other is usually older information, often metadiscourse. The older information, particularly metadiscourse, should come first. When it doesn't, we can often just reverse the order of subject and what follows the verb:

> *Those questions relating to the ideal system for providing instruction in home computers* are **just as confused.**

> **Just as confused** are *those questions relating to the ideal system for providing instruction in home computers.*

> *The need for closer monitoring of cash flow* is **the next problem we must deal with.**

> **The next problem we must deal with** is *the need for closer monitoring of cash flow.*

This reversal puts the connection with a previous sentence closer to that sentence: *Just as confused* . . . , *The next problem* . . . ; and it puts the newer and more important ideas closer to following sentences, the sentences that will elaborate on them: . . . *instruction in home computers,* . . . *monitoring of cash flow.*

The same sort of switch is possible with a few other kinds of sentences. They typically announce the appearance of a new agent or something roughly equivalent:

> *The most important information* appeared **at the bottom of the page.**
>
> **At the bottom of the page** appeared *the most important information.*
>
> *Some very tough theoretical issues* stand **behind these issues.**
>
> **Behind these issues** stand *some very tough theoretical issues.*

PASSIVES AGAIN

The passive is one of the most useful devices for switching old and new. Since we've spent a good deal of time on passives already, here's just one more example:

> This chemical waste disposal facility *was never inspected* by the director of engineering, the official responsible for certifying its safety. He *had been misinformed* by test results *sent* him by the contractors who had designed the system.

In the first sentence, *this chemical waste disposal facility* points to a previous sentence. The new information is who did not perform an important action. And who did not is named at the end of the first sentence, in the passive *by*-phrase: . . . *by the director of engineering*. . . . That person then becomes the old information at the beginning of the second sentence: **He** *had been misinformed* . . . , another sequence that requires a passive. And the important part of that sentence comes last—what he was misinformed by and then who misinformed him: . . . misinformed *by test results sent him by the contractors*. . . .
Compare the active version:

> The director of engineering, the official responsible for certifying the safety of this chemical waste disposal facility, never inspected it. Test results sent to him by the contractors who had designed the system misinformed him.

Incidentally, this principle of switching old and new usually supports another principle we've already discussed—arranging units from shorter to longer. We typically express the newer and more important information in the longer and more complex phrases, the older in a much shorter phrase, often just a pronoun. So when we arrange elements to meet the old-new principle, we will usually satisfy that shorter-longer principle, too.

Exercise 6-I

Edit these next sentences into more economical form, and then revise them so that they end on their strongest note. Try switching subjects and complements, changing actives and passives, shifting movable modifiers, and the like.

1. Several upper and lower eyelid reconstruction evaluation studies are presented with the aforementioned summary discussions for your general information, in addition.
2. The slow and insidious overgrowth of our basic belief system in the supremacy and importance of logical and rational processing mechanisms has to an almost complete degree sublimated mental intuition in mankind, however.
3. Overbuilding of suburban housing developments has led to the existence of extensive and widespread flooding and economic disaster in some parts of our country in recent years, it now seems clear.
4. The teacher who makes an assignment of a long final term paper at the end of the semester and who then gives only a grade at the end and nothing else such as a critical comment is a common complaint among people who take college courses.
5. Engine fuel lines and steam heating systems in the older-type coaches also have been known to become choked with frozen ice under these particular conditions.
6. Renting textbooks for basic required courses—such as mathematics, foreign languages, and English—whose textbooks do not experience change from year to year is possible and feasible, however.
7. The course of the war and the future of world history would be changed as a result of an event that occurred at about this same point in time.
8. The effective and economical disposal of product materials

that are not such that they are found to undergo biodegradation in the environmental ecological system is a matter of a different nature, we believe.

9. The focusing of attention on community issues that are real rather than the creation of a conversational environment which results in exhaustion in the discussion and definition of broad problem areas is of most usefulness, in the initiation of dialogue.

10. Guidelines set forth in the MLA style sheet and the NCTE guidelines for the nonsexist use of language should be adhered to by writers of papers, moreover.

11. With the fastest growing population in the region, DuPage County covers 338 square miles of land area beginning about 16 miles west of the Chicago loop.

12. An attorney who will feel a certain responsiveness to your needs and interests and who has the capability for translating your organizational problems into the most suitable legal form is your first step, it is clear.

BEGINNING WELL

The beginning of a sentence is more difficult to manage than its end. If a sentence starts out right, the end flows almost inevitably from what comes first. But beginning each new sentence forces new decisions on us. What goes at the beginning strongly determines how a reader will understand what follows. In beginning a sentence, we face several different tasks.

1. To connect the new sentence to the preceding one, we use cohesive and transitional devices such as *and, but, therefore, however, instead* and longer phrases and clauses like *in the first place, on the other hand, as a result.*

2. We tell our readers how to evaluate what follows with expressions such as *fortunately, perhaps, allegedly, it is important to note that, everyone knows.*

3. We orient our reader to what follows with some preliminary context: *for the most part, in many ways, under these circumstances, to a certain extent, politically speaking, from a practical point of view, in terms of.*

4. We typically set the time and place of an event: *at that time, later, on May 23, in Europe, between the two armies.*
5. We announce the topic of a sentence, either by naming it in the subject of a clause or by introducing it with phrases such as *in regard to, as for, turning now to, speaking of, as far as X is concerned.*

Cohesion and Transition

There's no consensus on how best to use connecting words like *therefore, however, nevertheless,* and *but, yet, so.* Some editors suggest that we should use many of them; others, few. Some competent writers use them frequently, others rarely. But however we use them, we ought to place them close to the beginning of their sentences, usually among the first six words. Here are some of the more common transitional devices:

• *Adding:* furthermore, in addition, moreover, similarly, and, also
• *Opposing:* but, however, though, nevertheless, on the other hand
• *Concluding:* so, therefore, for, as a result, consequently
• *Exemplifying:* for example, for instance, to illustrate, that is
• *Intensifying:* in fact, indeed, even, as a matter of fact
• *Sequencing:* first, second, finally, in conclusion, to sum up

  Adding: If you begin a sentence or a paragraph with *also, and,* or *another,* look closely. There is nothing intrinsically wrong with starting with *and,* but general connectors like these suggest that you may not have thought through the logical connections between your ideas, that you may be just adding one thought to another. *Also* at the beginning of a sentence can make it seem especially tacked-on:

> Metaphor is one of the most difficult figures of speech for an inexperienced writer to master. *Also,* irony can be a problem.

Be sure your *also* introduces a second item parallel to the preceding one, not an elaboration on the first:

> Metaphor is one of the most difficult figures of speech for an inexperienced writer to master. Also, it requires a mature imagination and a sense of appropriateness.

That *also* doesn't introduce something parallel to metaphor, but something that elaborates on it. *Because* would be more exact:

> . . . an inexperienced writer to master, *because* it requires a mature imagination and a sense of appropriateness.

And avoid beginning more than a few sentences with *and:* Reserve it for places where you want some special emphasis, usually toward the end of a sequence of things. You can use it to signal your reader that you have come to the last item in a series.

Opposing: Whenever you contradict or qualify a statement, signal the qualification early on with *but, however, on the other hand.* If you use *however,* try to put it immediately after the point you are contradicting:

> The members of the committee agreed on the policy they would follow in regard to late submissions. The chairman, *however,* warned that too strict a policy would be counterproductive.

When you begin a sentence with *but* or *however,* be sure you are introducing a real qualification and not just another thought. The *but* in this next example does not introduce a real qualification; it only signals a kind of "I-think-I'll-change-the-subject."

> The death penalty has never proved to be a significant deterrent to homicide. *But* it has been tested in the Supreme Court on several occasions as an inherently unfair penalty applied more often to the poor than to the rich.

If you put a comma before a *however,* be certain that the *however* is inside its own sentence. If the *however* introduces an independent clause*, either capitalize the *however* (after a period) or separate the *however* from what has gone before with a semicolon. *Not* this:

> The members of the committee agreed on the policy they would follow in regard to late *submissions, however, the applicants* were never informed.

But this:

> . . . follow in regard to late *submissions. However,* the applicants. . . .
> . . . follow in regard to late *submissions; however,* the applicants. . . .

A sequence of *but*s can be both confusing and awkward:

> The competition to discover the particular shape of the DNA chain came down to what looked like a dead heat between Linus Pauling and the Watson-Crick team, *but* it was the latter who had the decided advantage of far superior X-ray photographs. *But* even if Pauling had had the same pictures, he probably wouldn't have been able to look at them objectively because he was so committed to the concept of a triple helix.

You can avoid a second *but* with a *however:*

> The competition to discover the particular shape of the DNA chain came down to what looked like a dead heat between Linus Pauling and the Watson-Crick team. It was the latter, *however,* who had the decided advantage of far superior . . . .

You can also change that second *but* to a *though* and move it into its sentence a word or two:

> The competition to discover the particular shape of the DNA chain came down to what looked like a dead heat between Linus Pauling and the Watson-Crick team, but it was the latter who had the decided advantage of far superior x-ray photographs. Even if Pauling had had the same pictures, *though,* he probably wouldn't have been able . . . .

Concluding: Use logical connectors such as *therefore, hence, thus,* and *then* sparingly. The flow of your thought should be clear enough not to require them, except for special emphasis. Because they are so varied, it might be useful to review their exact meanings:

- *As a result:* The final consequence in a chain of events.
- *Consequently:* A peripheral or direct result but not necessarily the final one.
- *Therefore:* Introduces a step in a logical sequence, not in a causal one.
- *Thus, hence, then:* Close to *therefore.*
- *So:* Less formal than the others, and because it is less specific, it can replace most of them in a casual style.

Examples:

> The depreciation of the dollar against the mark has made German imports and German vacations increasingly expensive. *As a result,* products ranging from wine to automobiles are in danger of pricing themselves out of the middle-class American market.

> New right-to-privacy laws have made it impossible to compile health data in the ways we have been doing it. *Consequently,* we are no longer able to analyze the real needs of our students.

> Your application failed to indicate the financial resources of your family. We must *therefore* reject your application for scholarship aid.

A FINE POINT: Avoiding the Obvious

This is not really a fine point at all, but one so important to clarity and cohesion that it deserves a chapter to itself. It is, though, a matter less stylistic than conceptual, so I will only summarize it.

When we write, we do not, we *should* not, make explicit every logical connection between one sentence and the next:

> In America today, secondary schools are beginning to swing back to a greater concern for the basics, away from those transitory, topical interests that have been the staple of so many high-school elective programs. We can at least hope that, one day soon, college freshmen will no longer have to be taught how to spell or punctuate or how to divide fractions, even if it means they must forego learning the history of Superman comic books or the plot conventions of old-time Western serials.

In that passage I depend on you to fill in a good deal of information that is only implied: that secondary schools do not now teach basics; that among the basics are spelling, punctuation, and dividing fractions; that among the trendy, topical interests are Superman comic books and old-time Western serials; that secondary-school students become college freshmen; that college freshmen must now be taught the basics; that this is a bad thing; that the change is a good thing. None of this information is specifically stated, but most of us can infer it from this passage on the basis of what we know about schools, students, and the basics.

As we saw in Lesson 3, we become wordy when we make too much of this connecting tissue visible, when we state what our readers can infer:

> In America today, secondary schools have elective programs rather than required programs, and they do not teach basics such as spelling, punctuation, and dividing fractions. This is a bad thing. Instead, the schools are teaching transitory topics such as the history of Superman comic books and plot conventions from old time Western serials. Since this does not prepare students for college work, when they go to college they are unprepared. Because they do not know these basics, the colleges have to teach them. But some secondary schools are swinging away from those transitory topics and back to basics. If the students do learn those basics before they go to college, then the colleges will not have to teach them. And that is a good thing.

But if we leave out too much connecting tissue, our writing may seem disjointed and hard to follow:

> In America today, the secondary schools are beginning to swing away from subjects like the history of Superman comic books. Soon, college freshmen may no longer have to be taught the basics.

Unfortunately, I can't offer any simple rules for deciding when you are supplying too much connecting tissue and when you are leaving too much out. An audience that knows your subject very well may find even a little connecting tissue unnecessary and condescending. Another audience, one unfamiliar with your subject, may need a good deal. This problem of connecting tissue is simply one to be aware of, one whose solution depends more on a sensitivity to your audience than on any special stylistic skill.

Orienters

Orienters guide a reader through a sentence by establishing a point of view toward what follows them. They may set the time or place of events:

> *In the late nineteenth century,* English poetry entered a period of

uncertainty and change that would eventually transform it almost beyond recognition.

During the next few years, America must solve its balance of payments problem.

Orienters can also restrict the range or certainty of an assertion:

Under certain circumstances, it is possible to control one's own autonomic system.

Up to a point, we are all willing to follow orders without question.

And they can provide a point of view toward what follows:

From a political standpoint, Carter's efforts to bring peace to the Middle East were at best a risky undertaking.

Pragmatically, we would do better to decrease the size of the package than to raise its price.

Because orienters provide the context for an assertion, they are most helpful when we place them early in the sentence. When adverbs of time and degree, of point of view and cohesion, appear at the end of a sentence, they not only distract a reader from the appropriate stress but also force him to orient himself retrospectively, *after* he needs the orientation.

Topics

The topic* is what a sentence is about, flows from, comments on. In most sentences, the topic is the subject:

Food processors have become the most popular new kitchen convenience.

But if metadiscourse gets in the way, the topic can be an object:

Next, I would like to discuss *food processors,* the most popular new kitchen convenience.

A topic can also appear in an introductory phrase:

In regard to *abortion*, few issues have so excited the passions of supporters and opponents alike.

About the *religious cults* that seize young people, what is there to say except that they must be controlled?

In this paragraph, *the topics* are italicized: *Topics* are important because *they* focus a reader's attention on particular ideas toward the beginning of each clause. *These ideas* provide the reader with thematic signposts defining the sequence of major points. If *a sequence of topics* makes sense, *the reader* can move from one sentence to the next from a cumulatively coherent point of view. But if through a paragraph *the topics* shift randomly from idea to idea, *the reader* has to begin each sentence out of context, with no consistent background. *Whatever we announce as a topic,* then, will fix a reader's point of view, not just toward what immediately follows but to a whole section of a discourse. Compare this:

> In this next paragraph, *I*'ve put topics in italics: *Topics* are important because *the beginning of each clause* is a thematic signpost that focuses the reader's attention on a particular idea. If *some kind of sense* can be made from a coherent sequence of topics, then *a series of sentences* will move the reader through them from a cumulatively coherent point of view. If there is *a random shift* from idea to idea, *the beginning of each sentence* will provide no context, no consistent background for a reader.

This revised paragraph has a fuzzy, confused movement because the topics shift almost at random.

This principle of providing a coherent sequence of topics also explains why one long sentence after another can be cumulatively so confusing. Very long sentences don't let us announce topics often enough or stress important ideas often enough. A reader finds too few thematic signals to give him a clear direction through a discourse. And he has too few instances of stressed information to understand what is important.

The beginning of a sentence, then, can be a busy place—sometimes too busy:

> However, in recent years, because of the great increase in automobile repair costs, local governments are attempting to regulate . . . .

When a sentence begins as haltingly as that one, we ought to edit it:

> But because automobile costs have recently increased so much, local governments are attempting to regulate . . . .

SUMMING UP:
THE PRINCIPLES OF EMPHASIS AND COHESION

1. Emphasis.
   a. Put your most important ideas at the end of your sentence, and if your sentence has several clauses, arrange the ideas inside each clause so that the most important ones come last.
   b. Don't write all long or all short sentences. If you do, you will provide too few or too many points of emphasis.
2. Cohesion.
   a. Be certain that one idea logically follows another. Don't force your reader to construct a long chain of inferences between one sentence and the next.
   b. Within paragraphs, try to make your topics a coherent sequence of items. Don't hesitate to repeat the same subject through a series of consecutive sentences.
   c. Put at the end of a sentence the information that you intend to develop in the next sentence.
   d. Put connecting words such as *therefore, consequently, however,* close to the beginning of their sentences. Use logical connectors such as *so, therefore, then, thus* sparingly. Always signal a contradiction or qualification with *but, though, however, on the other hand.*
   e. Look twice at every *and* and *also* that opens a sentence.

The System of Clarity

By now, we can appreciate how extraordinarily complex a sentence really is. A sentence is more than its subject, verb, and object. It is more than its words. It is a multilevel system whose parts we can fit together in very delicate ways to achieve very precise ends—if we know how. We can match or mismatch the grammatical units and their related semantic meanings:

subject	verb	object
agent	action	goal

We can match or mismatch the rhetorical units and their meaning:

topic	stress
old/less important	new/more important

And we can fit these two systems together:

subject	verb	object
agent	action	goal
topic		stress
old/less important	new/more important	

Of course, you can't construct every sentence on this pattern. But when you write sentences that thoroughly and consistently depart from it, your prose will more often than not be confused, unclear, and imprecise. Follow it, and more often than not you will write a prose that is clear, coherent, and forceful.

Exercise 6-II

In the following units, edit to improve cohesive flow. (1) Move transitional devices and orienters to the beginning of their sentences; (2) arrange the order of topics so that they are logical. Generally edit the passages so that they are more economical and direct.

1. Analytic and normative criticism are the two modes that this kind of stylistic criticism comes in. That the best of all possible texts for the content it expresses is the text before us is the assumption of analytic criticism. To explain why the text is as it is is the only task of the analytic critic. Where the writer missed matching his language to his ideas

is explained by the normative critic, on the other hand. That the writer could have failed his intention is its assumption. The fame or obscurity of the author more than the intrinsic quality of a text determines which we choose.

2. A steady Darwinian selection has been imposed on the population of discontented Europeans by the discovery of America. A new chance to come here made the most intrepid and least rooted gladly give up everything. Staying put was the lot of the lazy, the fearful, the least discontented. Personality traits that led to an adventurous independence have always been favored by the gene pool that has constituted the American genetic heritage, as a result.

3. Vegetation covers the earth, except for those areas continuously covered with ice or utterly scorched by continual heat. Richly fertilized plains and river valleys are places where plants grow, as well as at the edge of perpetual snow in high mountains. There is plant growth not only in and around lakes and swamps but under the ocean and next to it. The cracks of busy city sidewalks have plants in them as well as in barren rocks. Before man existed the earth was covered with vegetation, and the earth will have vegetation long after evolutionary history swallows us up.

4. A concern with gesture and an awareness of the role of empty space in design can provide a definition of abstract expressionism. The work of many artists who rejected the unreal "reality" of philosophic realism has these qualities. Albert Cinque, whose "Study #A" is a play of delicate line against white parchment, is one such artist. With its stark existential spaces overwhelming the spidery yet assertive scrolls, the paper itself becomes part of the medium no less than the ink.

5. The power to create and communicate a new message to fit a new experience is not part of the power of animals in their natural states. Their genetic code imposes on them only what they can communicate. Information in regard to distance, direction, source richness, in regard to pollen,

constitutes the total information content which can be communicated by bees. The same limited repertoire of messages delivered over and over in the same way, for generation after generation, is characteristic of animals of the same species, in all significant respects, however.

Some Special Problems

Pedantry consists in the use of words unsuitable to the time, place, and company.

Samuel Taylor Coleridge

Clear writers, like fountains, do not seem so deep as they are; the turbid look the most profound.

Walter Savage Landor

From time to time, some of us have to write for an audience unable to understand easily anything but the clearest and simplest language possible. Or we may have to write on a subject so complex that even a competent reader will understand it only if we make it utterly direct and explicit. Everything we have said so far applies to either case—short sentences, short words, a minimum of clutter, a verbal rather than a nominal style.

AUDIENCE AS AGENT

When we write in this way for readers who do not read easily or quickly, we are often giving them immediately practical advice— how to do something like operate a machine, file a form, or rent a house. Or we may be trying to inform them about significant facts that directly affect them: about inflation, politics, or their health. For such readers, information that seems dissociated from their immediate experience can be too abstract to be meaningful, too distant to be relevant. We can make it immediately relevant by bringing our readers into the flow of the discourse, by making *them* agents* and goals*, and their experiences the action. Now, obviously, we can't do that when we write about experiences and events entirely separate from their lives. But when we write about subjects that do involve our readers, we can help them understand if we make them part of the discourse.

Here, for example, is some advice on consumerism that appeared in a publication directed to a very broad audience:

> The following information should be verified in every lease before signing: a full description of the premises to be rented and its exact location; the amount, frequency, and dates of payments; the amounts of deposits and pre-payments of rents; a statement setting forth the conditions under which the deposit will be refunded.

That's not particularly difficult for an educated adult. And we could make it clearer yet for an audience that reads less easily if we use all the editorial tactics we've discussed so far. But to make it clear and comprehensible for an audience that may find *any* kind of writing difficult, we can also rewrite from the point of view of that audience (emphasis added):

When *you* get the lease from the landlord, don't sign it right away. Before *you* sign, look for these things:

1. Does the lease describe the place that *you* are renting?

2. Does the lease tell *you* exactly where that place is?

3. Does the lease tell *you* how much rent money *you* have to pay? Does it tell *you* how often *you* have to pay it? Does it tell *you* on what day *you* have to pay it?

4. Does the lease say how much deposit money *you* have to give to the landlord before *you* move in? Does it say how much rent *you* have to give him before *you* move in?

5. Does the lease tell *you* when the landlord can keep *your* deposit money and not give it back to *you*?

We've done more than shorten sentences*, use simple words, and put agents into subjects* and actions into verbs*. Just as important, we've made the reader's experience part of the discourse. (We've also used a tabular order with lots of white space. Had it been longer, we could have broken it up with headings and subheadings.)

Now, if our revision is more accessible than the original, it's also longer. But we ought not assume that it is less economical—at least not if we judge economy by a measure more sophisticated than mere number of words. The real measure of economy should be whether we have achieved our ends, whether our readers understand what we want them to do and then do it.

Here is another example that might make the point clearer. It is an excerpt from an actual set of regulations intended to tell train crews how to keep one train from running into another:

When a train is moving on a main track at less than one-half the maximum authorized timetable speed for any train at that location, under circumstances in which it may be overtaken, a crew member must put off single burning fusees at rear of train at intervals that do not exceed the burning time of the fusee.

When a train is moving on a main track at or more than one-half the maximum authorized timetable speed for any train at that location, under circumstances in which it may be overtaken, crew members responsible for providing protection must consider grade, track curvature, weather conditions, sight distance, and speed of the train relative to following trains, when deciding if burning fusees should be put off.

Those two sentences have only three passives*, five harmless nominalizations*, and relatively little clutter. But at fifty-seven and sixty-six words, they are far too long and too packed with information to be clear to a trainman who may never have gone beyond the ninth grade. Indeed, they are a bit much for any reader. This would be clearer:

> When you are responsible for your train, and you think another train might overtake you, you must put off burning fusees from the rear of your train. Follow these guidelines:
>
> *Condition #1:* Your train is on a main track, and it is moving at *less* than half the speed that the timetable allows for any train at that location.
>
> —You must put off single burning fusees at periods of time that are shorter than the time it takes for each fusee to burn out.
>
> *Condition #2:* Your train is on a main track, and it is moving at *more* than half the speed that the timetable allows for any train at that location.
>
> —You must consider these conditions when you put off fusees.
>
> —grade
> —sight distance
> —track curvature
> —weather conditions
> —speed of your train compared to the speed of a following train

I've broken two long sentences into smaller, more comprehensible ones. I've laid the directions out in more space. I've also used a few more words—fourteen. Does that make this version less economical? Not if we balance the cost of the paper against the cost of a couple of trains. Short-term savings don't always mean long-run economy. (In fact, anyone can read the longer version faster than the shorter one as well as understand it better.)

We can often recast even the most abstract discourse in this way. Here is an excerpt from an article by Talcott Parsons, a social scientist who was notorious for his opaque style:

Apart from theoretical conceptualization there would appear to be no method of selecting among the indefinite number of varying kinds of factual observation which can be made about a concrete phenomenon or field so that the various descriptive statements about it articulate into a coherent whole, which constitutes an "adequate," a "determinate" description. Adequacy in description is secured in so far as determinate and verifiable answers can be given to all the scientifically important questions involved. What questions are important is largely determined by the logical structure of the generalized conceptual scheme which, implicitly or explicitly, is employed.

If we edit this passage in all the ways we've discussed so far and recast it from the point of view of the reader, we can make it considerably more accessible, at least to a moderately well educated audience:

If you don't have a theory, you don't have a way to select from among all the things you could say about something just those things that would fit into a coherent whole, a whole that would be "adequate" or "determinate." You describe something "adequately" only when you can verify your answers to questions that scientists think are important. And they decide what questions are important on the basis of the theories that they implicitly or explicitly use.

And even that could be made more direct:

If you want to describe something so that what you say about it fits into a coherent whole, you need a theory. When you ask a question, you have to have a theory to verify your answers. The theory that you use even determines the questions you ask.

Should anyone claim that I have lost subtle nuances of Parsons's argument, I would have to acknowledge that all the qualifications don't appear in the simplest version. On the other hand, the excruciating syntax in Parsons's original must obscure those nuances from all but the most masochistically dedicated reader.

I am not suggesting that the style we're describing here is the sine qua non of good writing. In the next lesson, we'll discuss some reasons for choosing artful complexity over utter directness. But large numbers of adults are less than entirely competent readers: By one estimate, one out of every five American adults is functionally illiterate. If so, then another must be almost as incompetent. That fact should disconcert a society increasingly dependent on information. We can agree to deplore the need to write in a manner so condescendingly simple. But if we translate our regret into a principled refusal to write in a way that may seem to some unacceptably simple, we risk letting one train slam into another.

Exercise 7-I

Rewrite these passages according to the directions.

1. This is an excerpt from an actual recall letter sent to an automobile owner. Rewrite it so that anyone who received the letter would respond.

   A defect which involves the possible failure of a frame support plate may exist on your vehicle. This plate (front suspension pivot bar support plate) connects a portion of the front suspension to the vehicle frame, and its failure could affect vehicle directional control, particularly during heavy brake application. In addition, your vehicle may also require adjustment service to the hood secondary catch system. The secondary catch may be misaligned so that the hood may not be adequately restrained to prevent hood fly-up in the event the primary latch is inadvertently left unengaged. Sudden hood fly-up beyond the secondary catch while driving could impair driver visibility. In certain circumstances, occurrence of either of the above conditions could result in vehicle crash without prior warning.

2. This is from Section 3102 of the Internal Revenue Code. It has to do with paying Social Security taxes for employees. Rewrite this so that someone who had hired a baby-sitter a few days a week would understand the provision and comply with the law rather than fire the baby-sitter out of sheer frustration.

   The tax imposed by section 3101 shall be collected by the employer of the taxpayer, by deducting the amount of the tax from the wages as and when paid. An employer who in any calendar quarter pays to an employee cash remuneration to which paragraph (7) (B) or (C) or (10) of section 3121 (a) is applicable may deduct an amount equivalent to such tax from any such payment of remuneration, even though at the time of payment the total amount of such remuneration paid to the employee by the employer in the calendar quarter is less than $50; and an employer who in any calendar year pays to an employee cash remuneration to which paragraph (8) (B) of section 3121(a) is applicable may deduct an amount equivalent to such tax from any such payment of remuneration, even though at the time of payment the total amount of such remuneration paid to the employee by the employer in the calendar year is less than $150 and the employee has not performed agricultural labor for the employer on 20 days or more in the calendar year for cash remuneration computed on a time basis.

3. Here are excerpts from two insurance policies. Rewrite both so that anyone who can read can understand them. The first step is to break the sentences into shorter grammatical sentences.

(a) The words "damages because of bodily injury by accident or disease including death at any time resulting therefrom" includes damages for care and loss of services and damages due to insurer liability by reason of suits or claims brought against the insured by others for the recovery of damages obtained from such others because of such bodily injury sustained by employees of the insured arising out of and in the course of their employment.

(b) If the Insured Person, while insured under this Policy, experiences whole and continuous disability by reason of accidental injury or by reason of sickness, and is thereby prevented on account of such disability from the performance of each and every duty of his occupation, and each and every duty of all other occupations and business for remuneration or profit, for a period of more than thirty consecutive days, the Company will pay to the Policyholder or the Bank, as irrevocable creditor-beneficiary, for each day in such period on which such person remains so disabled, commencing with the thirty-first day of such period, a Daily Benefit determined in accordance with the provision entitled "Amount of Benefit" contained herein; provided, however, that the liability of the Company under the Disability Benefit is limited to payment of such benefits for a period of not more than eighteen months in connection with any one period of continuous disability. If the Insured Person suffers a recurrent disability arising out of the same cause or causes of a previous disability before the expiration of six consecutive months after the date of termination of such previous period of disability, the liability of the Company in connection with such subsequent period of disability shall be limited to the remaining portion of said eighteen-month period of benefits not exhausted during such prior period or periods of disability.

SPECIFIC AND CONCRETE

Regardless of our audience, we can make writing readable and memorable by writing specifically and concretely. When we squeeze long, windy phrases into more compact phrases, we make diffuse ideas sharply specific:

> As the number of people in our population between the ages of about eighteen to twenty-two who successfully complete their high-school education becomes smaller, institutions of higher education supported by private funds will experience increasing difficulties in maintaining the number of students enrolled at a level that will result in the continuing high quality of higher education.

Compare:

> As high-school graduates become fewer, private colleges will find it more difficult to keep their enrollments high enough to offer quality education.

We can also be more concrete—and therefore more memorable—if we replace general words with words that are more specific. Words come in sets. Some constitute a set of equally general things:

> poodle   collie   beagle   setter

Others constitute a set that ranges from very specific and narrow to very general:

Sam   beagle   hound   dog   canine   animal   creature

Each more general member includes all those that precede it. *Sam,* for me, unambiguously names a single entity. *Beagle* can name Sam along with hundreds of thousands of other dogs, *hound* all of those and more, *dog* even more. *Canine* includes all the dogs, wolves, coyotes, and dingos of the world; *animal,* all of those plus millions more; and *creature,* more yet.

The more narrow the reference, the more concrete the idea; the more concrete the idea, the clearer and more precise the idea. To be very specific, we sometimes need more, not fewer words:

> Officials were unable to account for money spent.

> George Smith and William Winston, president and comptroller of Amtex Industries, could not explain what happened to $452,983, which they had spent on food services.

> Students who choose to major in a science here must be mathematically competent.

> Sophomores who choose to major in physics, chemistry, or geology at Southwestern U. must demonstrate that they can do calculus through differential equations.

> There must be improvements in the characteristics of our larger motors in the near future.

> Within six months, the engineering staff must design any engine over 500 horsepower to operate not two months without servicing, but four.

The more general sentences could serve as introductory statements, as topic sentences to paragraphs. Concreteness usually becomes a problem after the topic sentence. The worst writers go on writing in that same abstract way.

At some point, of course, concrete and specific language becomes superfluous detail. At what point depends on the situation. Generally, writers with little authority (the young, the inexperienced, the unreliable, the unknown) need to furnish more detailed evidence to be persuasive than those with established reputations.

A FINE POINT: The Representative Example

There is a style that typically uses the specific to stand for the general. Compare,

> Our students' mental health depends on their occasionally taking a break from their studies and relaxing.

> Our students' mental health depends on their occasionally closing their Aristotle and opening a Schlitz.

> Wasting fuel on unnecessary driving is a sure way to guarantee that we will not have sufficient heating oil next winter.

> Driving your Cadillac two blocks to the local Burger King is a sure way to guarantee that all of us will have chattering teeth next January.

We know that *Aristotle* stands for all studies, *Schlitz* for relaxation, *driving a Cadillac two blocks*, etc., for unnecessary driving. We could have used *Descartes* and *Pabst*, *Lincoln* and *Kentucky Fried Chicken*, *be wearing three sweaters* and *February*, and still have communicated essentially the same message.

This kind of specific diction invests a style with a nervous energy that finally can become a bit exhausting. Just as we need an occasional short sentence—or long one—to establish a flexible rhythm, so the rhythm of concrete and abstract, specific and general, needs the same kind of flexibility.

Exercise 7-II

Here are some very general sentences. Rewrite them so that you communicate the same idea through specific and concrete images. For example:

> Many sports heroes expect too much, a situation that ordinary fans won't support much longer.

If the Richy Allens and the Larry Birds keep demanding a half million a year and interest-free loans, then the Joe Doakses are going to start turning off the TV.

1. Some politicians spend our taxes on useless projects.
2. People who live in big cities on the East Coast are generally threatened by street crime.
3. These days, most movies seem out to scare us.
4. Rock groups are becoming more concerned with showmanship than music.
5. Because of fuel shortages, many of us are taking vacations closer to home.
6. Some books bore me.
7. Production-line workers are becoming more interested in nonmonetary rewards for their labor.
8. You don't get very many nutritious components in most breakfast cereals.

LOGICAL ORDER

When you are giving directions for a task that requires more than one or two steps, it's particularly important to be as clear and as specific as possible. Before you begin to write, list the steps in the precise order in which they must be performed. Then group them into "islands" of steps, groups of steps that constitute a larger phase or logical stages in the process. Then do the same with the islands: Group them into still larger units. In a very complex task involving a great many steps, you may even have to group the groups again.

For example, here's a list of practical steps for checking and revising your style:

1. Find phrases that you can replace with a single word.
2. Cross out whatever interrupts subject-verb and move it before the subject.
3. Circle verbs. Revise so that the crucial actions are in verbs.
4. Put a wavy line under the last few words in every sentence. If they do not express the most significant information, find that information and put it last.

5. Cross out all metadiscourse. Reread, restoring only what you must.
6. Underline all subjects. If sequences in paragraphs do not form coherent groups, create subjects that would, and make them subjects.
7. Make a slash between every grammatical sentence*. If most exceed thirty words, break the longest into shorter sentences; if most have fewer than fifteen words, combine some into longer ones.
8. Put a *T* over all transitional words to make sure they are among the first five or six words in their sentences.
9. Put an *A* over the agent of each action. If most significant actions seem to lack express agents or if the agents are infrequently the subjects of the verbs that name their actions, revise the sentence to make those agents subjects. Create agents where appropriate.
10. Read each sentence, dropping every word and phrase that isn't necessary to your meaning.
11. Compare the length of your subjects and complements*, and try revising when you find subjects significantly longer than complements.
12. Look for strings of compound nouns. Rewrite any that you have invented into noun + prepositional phrase*.
13. Try turning every negative into an affirmative.
14. Put an *O* over every orienter*, and try moving it to the beginning of its sentence.

That list has no internal coherence; it is a collection of seemingly unrelated items in no logical sequence. Our first step in revising that list is to put together what goes together, then order the items into a logical sequence. The second step is to write a sentence that will summarize the point and function of each stage and, if necessary, a sentence or two that summarizes series of stages. This gives you a synopsis and outline of the stages of the process, an overview of the whole process.

If we did that with this list of fourteen items, we would have something we could more easily recall:

To edit your writing, you must do the following: (1) Eliminate all wordiness. (2) Consistently match your subjects, agents, and topics;

match verbs and actions; match ends of your sentences and your most significant information. (3) Move to the beginning of your sentences what belongs there. (4) Break up sentences that are too long and combine sentences that are too short.

1. *Eliminate all wordiness that does not require you to significantly recast your sentence.*
    a. Read each sentence, dropping every word and phrase that isn't necessary to your meaning.
    b. Cross out all metadiscourse, and then reread, restoring only what you must.
    c. Find sequences of words that you can replace with single words.
    d. Look for strings of compound nouns, and rewrite any you have invented into noun + prepositional phrase.
    e. Try turning every negative into an affirmative.

2. *Examine your sentences to determine how consistently you have expressed significant actions in verbs, agents and topics in subjects, and significant information in stresses.*
    a. Circle each verb. If it does not express a significant action, find the most significant action and make it a verb.
    b. Put an *A* over the agent of each action. If most significant actions seem to lack express agents, or if the agents are infrequently the subjects of verbs that name their actions, revise the sentence to make those agents subjects. Create agents where appropriate.
    c. Underline all subjects. If sequences of subjects in paragraphs do not form coherent groups, create subjects that would.
    d. Put a wavy line under the last words in every sentence. If they do not express the most significant new information, find that information, and put it last.
    e. Compare the length of subjects and complements; when you find subjects significantly longer than complements, try revising.

3. *Move to the beginning of your sentences what should go there:*
    a. Put an *O* over every orienter; try to move it to the beginning of its sentence.
    b. Put a *T* over all transitional words. If they are not

among the first five or six words in their sentence, try
to move them there.
   c. Cross out whatever interrupts the subject-verb, and
   move it before the subject.
4. *Break up sentences that are too long and combine sentences that
   are too short.*
   a. Make a slash mark between every grammatical sentence.
   b. If most exceed thirty words, try breaking them into
   shorter sentences.
   c. If most sentences are shorter than fifteen words, try
   combining them into longer ones.
   d. Go back and redo steps 1–4.

You now have four large chunks to hold in mind, each chunk
comprising no more than five smaller chunks. The larger chunks
and the smaller chunks are in a logical sequence in which each step
builds on a previous step. The headings sum up the chunks, and the
general heading sums up the headings of the chunks.

SUMMING UP: THE MATTER OF SPECIAL CLARITY

1. Style
   a. Put your audience into the sentence as subject-agents or
   object-goals.
   b. Make their crucial actions verbs.
   c. Keep your sentences relatively short, from fifteen to
   eighteen words.
   d. Use words that are concrete, specific; use few abstract
   nouns.
   e. Put important information at the end of your sentences,
   never buried in the middle; keep your topics consistent.
2. Form
   a. Order information in a way that reflects a "natural"
   order, usually chronological.
   b. Chunk information, and introduce chunks with
   summaries in the form of topic sentences or summary
   overviews.

3. Logic
    a. Signal all oppositions or qualifications with *but, however,* etc.
    b. Make all cause-effect relationships self-evident.
    c. Rely little on implied information; make everything explicit.

Lesson Eight

A Touch of Class

Anything is better than not to write clearly. There is nothing to be said against lucidity, and against simplicity only the possibility of dryness. This is a risk well worth taking when you reflect how much better it is to be bald than to wear a curly wig.

Somerset Maugham

But clarity and brevity, though a good beginning, are only a beginning. By themselves, they may remain bare and bleak. When Calvin Coolidge, asked by his wife what the preacher had preached on, replied "Sin," and, asked what the preacher had said, replied "He was against it," he was brief enough. But one hardly envies Mrs. Coolidge.

F. L. Lucas

There are two sorts of eloquence; the one indeed scarce deserves the name of it, which consists chiefly in laboured and polished periods, an over-curious and artificial arrangement of figures, tinselled over with a gaudy embellishment of words, which glitter, but convey little or no light to the understanding. . . . The other sort of eloquence is quite the reverse to this, and which may be said to be the true characteristic of the holy Scriptures; where the eloquence does not arise from a laboured and far-fetched elocution, but from a surprising mixture of simplicity and majesty, which is a double character, so difficult to be united, that it is seldom to be met with in compositions merely human.

Laurence Sterne

Let's assume that you can now write clear, cohesive, and appropriately emphatic prose. That in itself would constitute a style of such singular distinction that most of us would be more than satisfied to achieve so much. But even though we might prefer bald clarity to the complexity of most institutional prose, the unrelenting simplicity of the plain style can finally become very flat and dry indeed, eventually arid. Its plainness invests prose with the blandness of unsalted meat and potatoes—honest fare to be sure, but hardly memorable and certainly without zest. Sometimes a touch of class, a flash of elegance, can mark the difference between forgettable Spartan plainness and a well-turned phrase that fixes itself in the mind of a reader.

Now, I can't tell you how to be graceful and elegant in the same way I can tell you how to be clear and direct. What I *can* do is tell you about some of the devices that some graceful writers use. But that advice is, finally, about as useful as listing the ingredients a great cook uses in his bouillabaisse and then expecting anyone to make it. Knowing the ingredients and knowing how to use them is the difference between reading cookbooks and Cooking.

What follows describes a few ingredients of a modestly elegant style. How imaginatively and skillfully you use them is the difference between reading this book on writing, and Writing.

BALANCE AND SYMMETRY

We've already described coordination* as one device for extending the movement of a sentence* beyond a few words. Coordination itself will grace a sentence with a movement more rhythmic and satisfying than that of a noncoordinate sentence. Compare:[1]

> Cheesecake TV such as "Charlie's Angels" and "Three's Company" appeals to men who need the stimulation of beautiful bodies. Women like them because they long for the energy those bodies represent and their freedom.

---

[1] The curly braces will signal a *coordinated* set of words, phrases, or clauses.

"Three's Company" appeals

to men who need the stimulation of beautiful bodies

and

to women who long for the

energy

and

freedom those bodies represent.

We can enhance the grace and rhythm of coordination if we keep in mind a few simple principles. First, a coordinate series will move more gracefully if each succeeding coordinate member is longer than the one before it. So if you coordinate within a coordination, try to do it in the second member. Compare these:

> The Sunbelt of southwestern states will continue to attract new businesses looking for a low-salaried pool of nonunionized labor and cheap energy, and retirees looking for sunshine.

Schematically:

The Sunbelt of southwestern states will continue to attract

new businesses looking for

a low-salaried pool of nonunionized labor and cheap energy,

and

retirees looking for sunshine.

Compare:

> The Sunbelt of southwestern states will continue to attract retirees looking for sunshine, and new businesses looking for cheap energy and a low-salaried pool of nonunionized labor.

Schematically:

The Sunbelt of southwestern
states will continue to attract

{ retirees looking for sunshine,

and

new businesses looking for { cheap energy

and

a low-salaried pool of
nonunionized labor.

In the second, the parallels move from shorter to longer,
creating a rhythmically more attractive line.

We can use correlative conjunctions* such as *both X and Y, not only
X but also Y, neither X nor Y* to announce a balanced coordination and
heighten its dramatic impact. Compare these

The national
significance of an ethnic
minority depends upon
a sufficiently deep
historical identity that
makes it

{ impossible that the majority will
absorb the minority

and

inevitable that
the minority will { maintain its
identity

and
transmit its
heritage.

The national
significance of an ethnic
minority depends upon
a sufficiently deep
historical identity that
makes it

{ *not only* impossible that the majority
will absorb the minority

but

inevitable that
the minority will { *both* maintain its
identity
and
transmit its
heritage.

The second is clearly stronger than the first.

You can make these coordinate patterns even more rhetorically elegant if you consciously balance the internal parts of phrases* and clauses* against one another:

Neither { the vacuous emotion of daytime soap opera
nor
the mindless eroticism of nighttime sitcoms

reflects the best { that American artists are able to create
or
that American audiences are willing to support.

The richest kind of balance and parallelism counterpoints both grammar and meaning: here *vacuous* is balanced against *mindless, emotion* against *eroticism, daytime* against *nighttime, soap opera* against *sitcoms, artists* against *audiences, able* against *willing,* and *create* against *support.*

You can achieve the same effect when you balance against each other parts of sentences that are *not* coordinated. Here is a subject* balanced against an object*:

[*Scientists who tear down established views of the universe*
invariably challenge
those of us who have built up our visions of reality upon
those views.

Here, the predicate* of a relative clause* in a subject is balanced against the predicate* of that subject (the square brackets signal a balanced but *not* coordinate pair):

A government that is unwilling to
[*listen to the moderate voices of its citizenry*
must eventually answer to the harsh justice of its revolutionaries.

A direct object balanced against the object of a preposition:

Those of us who are vitally concerned about our failing school systems are not quite ready to sacrifice

> [*the intellectual growth of our innocent children*
>   *to*
> [*the social daydreaming of irresponsible bureaucrats.*

A main clause* against a subordinate clause*, and then a direct object and two prepositional objects against one another:

Were [*I trading* [*my scholarly principles*
        for
      [*financial security*

   [*I would scarcely be writing* [*short books*
               on
            minor subjects
             for
           small audiences.

None of these are coordinated, but they are all very consciously balanced. Like every other artful device, these balanced phrases and clauses can eventually become self-defeating—or at least monotonously arch. But if you can use them unobtrusively, when you want to emphasize an important point or conclude the line of an argument, you can give your prose a shape and a cadence that most ordinary writing lacks.

Exercise 8-I.

Pick five or six sentences that have been laid out schematically in this lesson or in any of the previous lessons and imitate their structural patterns. Don't try to imitate the sentences word for word or even phrase for phrase, but do try to follow the general structural pattern that we've discussed. For example, here's a sentence with a second coordination in the object:

A contemplative life in the country
{ requires the energy to overcome the brute facts of an
 uncooperative Nature
    but
{ rewards the person who has that energy

{ with the unmatchable satisfaction of having done it
            and
with an inner confidence that makes contemplation
    meaningful.

First, think of a subject close enough to this one to make your imitation easy—for example, the academic life:

Life as a college professor
{ offers summer vacations longer than most
            but
imposes a sense of guilt on that person who
        { ignores his or her scholarly work
                    and
        enjoys the time the profession offers.

Try laying out your sentence in the way the model is schematically arranged, but then write it out in the usual way, so that you can get the feel of a long sentence as it unfolds before you.

Some of the sentences you might imitate are on pages 81, 142–145.

Here are the first halves of some balanced sentences. Finish them so that the last half balances against the first half.

1. Those who keep silent over the loss of small freedoms . . .
2. While the strong are never afraid to admit their real weaknesses, the weak . . .
3. We should pay more attention to those politicians who tell us how to make what we have better than to those . . .
4. When parents raise children who do not value the importance of hard work, the adults those children become . . .
5. Too many teachers mistake neat papers rehashing conventional ideas for . . .

In these next exercises, you have only the pattern. You invent the material. Use other verbs, if they allow you to imitate the pattern.

6. trade X for Y (for example: I would never *trade* an immediate but transitory pleasure *for* a distant but enduring virtue.)

7. mistake X for Y
8. substitute X for Y
9. balance X against Y
10. sell X for Y

EMPHASIS AND RHYTHM

Emphasis, as we have seen, is largely a matter of controlling the way a sentence ends. When we maneuver into that stressed position our most important information, the natural emphasis we hear in our mind's ear underscores the rhetorical emphasis of a significant idea. Even that natural stress, though, can seem weak and anticlimactic if we let a sentence end on lightweight words.

Different parts of speech carry different weights. Prepositions are very light, one reason why we sometimes want to avoid leaving a preposition at the end. Sentences should move toward strength; ending with a preposition can dilute that strength. Compare:

> The intellectual differences among races is a subject that only the most politically indifferent scientist *is willing to look **into**.*

> The intellectual differences among races is a subject that only the most politically indifferent scientist *is willing to **explore**.*

Adjectives and adverbs are heavier than prepositions, but lighter than verbs and nouns. The heaviest, the most emphatic words, are nominalizations*, those nouns derived from verbs and adjectives. So if you want to end a sentence, or even a clause inside a sentence, with the greatest emphasis, end it with a nominalization or with a phrase centered on a nominalization.

Compare these, the first version by Somerset Maugham:

> You would have thought that men who passed their lives in the study of the great masters of literature would be sufficiently sensitive to the beauty of language to write if not beautifully at least with perspicuity.

> You would have thought that men who passed their lives studying the great masters of literature would be sufficiently sensitive to beautiful language to write about it if not beautifully at least perspicuously.

In the second version, we've changed the indirect abstract nominalizations to verbs, adjectives, and adverbs, words more immediate and direct—but at great cost to the concluding rhythm of the sentence. In Maugham's original, each major segment ends with a phrase built around a nominalization:

> in the *study* of the great masters of literature
>
> to the *beauty* of language
>
> with *perspicuity*

Another example: Which version is from Winston Churchill's "Finest Hour" speech is obvious.

> until in God's good time, the New World, with all its power and might, steps forth to the rescue and the liberation of the old.

> until in God's good time, the New World, with all its power and might, steps forth to rescue and liberate the old.

The second is weak, banal, pedestrian.

In fact, artfully placed nominalizations can elevate an otherwise flat style to one with a touch of elegance. Compare these two passages; one of them, from his *Memoirs,* is George Kennan's description of Averell Harriman. Which better reflects Harriman's own elegance is obvious:

> He had that curious contempt for elegance that only the wealthy can normally afford . . . in Moscow, [his] interest was, properly and commendably, the prospering of the American war effort and American diplomacy as President Roosevelt viewed and understood it. To the accomplishment of his part in the furtherance of this objective he addressed himself with a dedication, a persistence, and an unflagging energy and attention that has no parallel in my experience. . . . His physical frame, spare and sometimes ailing, seemed at best an unwelcome irrelevance. I had the impression that it was with an angry impatience that he took cognizance of the occasional reminders of its existence, dragged it with him on his daily rounds of duty, and forced it to support him where continuation without its support was not possible.

He had that curious contempt for elegant things that only wealthy people can normally afford . . . in Moscow, [he] was interested, properly and commendably, only in helping to prosper the American war effort and American diplomacy as President Roosevelt viewed and understood it. To accomplish his part in this objective he addressed himself in a dedicated and persistent way, with an unflagging energy and attention that parallels nothing I have experienced. . . . His physical frame, spare and sometimes ailing, seemed at best unwelcome and irrelevant. It seemed to me that he was angrily impatient when he recognized those times when it reminded him that it existed, dragged it with him on his daily rounds of duty, and forced it to support him where he could not have continued if it had not supported him.

Now, when a writer combines nominalizations with parallel constructions, even redundantly parallel constructions, we know he is cranking up a style that is openly aiming at elegant complexity. This sentence written by Walter Lippmann is a good example:

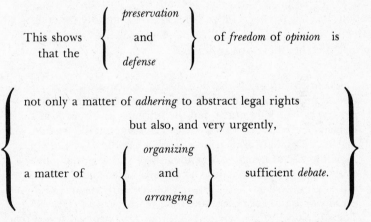

Compare the less redundant, but also the less elegant and rhythmically flatter,

This shows that if we want to preserve free opinion, we must adhere to abstract legal rights and very urgently organize it so that we can debate issues sufficiently.

There is another, rather small but important point of elegance: If we seek an *extravagantly* elegant style, we can end many of our sentences with phrases introduced by *of*. Many result from nominalizations:

the preservation and defense *of freedom of opinion*

but many do not—for example, phrases like those that end each major phrase in the opening sentence of Edward Gibbon's *Decline and Fall of the Roman Empire:*

In the second century *of the Christian era,* the empire *of Rome* comprehended the fairest part *of the earth,* and the most civilized portion *of mankind.*

Compare:

In the second century after Christ, the Roman Empire comprehended the earth's fairest part and most civilized people.

Gibbon, in fact, perhaps more consistently than any other English writer, combines all the devices of elegance that we've described (coordinate members are in italic):

It was scarcely possible that the eyes **of** contemporaries should discover in the public felicity the latent *causes of decay and corruption.* This long peace, and the uniform government **of** the Romans, introduced a slow and secret poison into *the vitals of the Empire.* The minds **of** men were gradually reduced to the same level, the fire **of** genius was extinguished, and even the military spirit evaporated. The natives **of** Europe were *brave and robust.* Spain, Gaul, Britain, and Illyricum supplied the regions with excellent soldiers, *and* constituted the real *strength of the monarchy.* Their personal valor remained, but they no longer possessed that public courage which is nourished by *the love of independence, the sense* **of** *national honor, the presence* **of** *danger, and the habit* **of** *command.* They *received laws and governors from the will of their sovereign, and trusted for their defence to a mercenary army.* The posterity **of** their boldest leaders was contented with the *rank of citizens and subjects.* The most aspiring spirits resorted to the *court or standard of the emperors;* and the deserted provinces, deprived **of** political strength or union, insensibly sunk into the languid indifference **of** private life.

One has but to recast a few of these sentences to recognize the points of style around which Gibbon crafts his elegantly Augustan prose: Change the climactic nominalizations to verbs and adjectives, condense the prepositional phrases to shorter noun phrases, prune the redundant doublets and self-conscious coordinations—and you have a style that is plain, sturdy, dry, and flat.

The secret to this kind of rhythmic elegance is to avoid piling up a series of lumbering nouns, without at the same time creating a clanking chain of prepositional phrases. This is too heavy:

> It was possible that contemporaries' eyes should discover in the public's felicity corruption's latent causes. This long, peaceful, uniform Roman government introduced slow secret poison into the Empire's vitals. Men's minds were gradually reduced to the same level, extinguishing genius's fire, and even the military spirit evaporated.

But this has too many prepositional phrases:

> It was scarcely possible that the eyes of contemporaries should discover in the felicity of the public the latent causes of decay and corruption. The length of the peace and the uniformity of the government of the Romans introduced a slow and secret poison into the vitals of the Empire of Rome. The minds of men were gradually reduced to a level of sameness, the fire of genius was extinguished, and even the spirit of the military evaporated.

We've exchanged the clumsiness of thump-thump-thump for the monotony of thumpity-thumpity-thump. Gibbon found his mean. Practice and an educated ear will help you find yours.

Exercise 8-II

In addition to suffering from several other faults, these next sentences end on weak adjectives and adverbs or clumsy possessives. Change them so that they end on more heavily stressed words, particularly on prepositional phrases beginning with *of*. For example:

> Our interest in ESP, UFOs, and other paranormal phenomena testifies to the fact that we have empty spirits and shallow minds.

Our interest in ESP, UFOs, and other paranormal phenomena testifies to the emptiness of our spirits and the shallowness of our minds.

1. Not very many tendencies in our governmental system have brought about more changes in American daily life than federal governmental agencies that are very powerful.
2. In the year 1923, several of the representatives from the side of the victorious Allied nations went to Versailles with the intention of seeking to dismember Germany's economic potential and to destroy her armaments industry.
3. The day is eliminated when school systems' boards of education have the expectation that local area taxpayers will automatically go along with whatever extravagant things administrators decide to do.
4. The blueprint for the political campaign plan was concocted by the mayor's advisers who are least sensitive.
5. If we invest our sweat in these projects, we must avoid appearing to be working only because we are interested in ourselves.
6. Irreplaceable works of native art are progressing into slow deterioration in many of our most prestigious museums for the reason that their curators have no recognition of how extremely fragile even recent artifacts can be.
7. Throughout history, science has made progress because dedicated scientists have gotten around a hostile public that is uninformed.

LENGTH AND RHYTHM

In ordinary functional prose, the length of your sentences becomes an issue only if they are all about fifteen words long, or if they are all much longer, over thirty or so. Though one eighteen-to-twenty-word sentence after another isn't the ideal goal, they will seem less obviously monotonous than a series of sentences that are regularly and significantly longer or shorter.

In artful prose, on the other hand, length is more deliberately controlled. Some accomplished stylists can write one short sentence after another, perhaps to suggest a note of urgency:

Toward noon Petrograd again became the field of military action; rifles and machine guns rang out everywhere. It was not easy to tell who was shooting or where. One thing was clear; the past and the future were exchanging shots. There was much casual firing; young boys were shooting off revolvers unexpectedly acquired. The arsenal was wrecked. . . . Shots rang out on both sides. But the board fence stood in the way, dividing the soldiers from the revolution. The attackers decided to break down the fence. They broke down part of it and set fire to the rest. About twenty barracks came into view. The bicyclists were concentrated in two or three of them. The empty barracks were set fire to at once.

—Leon Trotsky, *The Russian Revolution*
trans. by Max Eastman

Or terse certainty:

The teacher or lecturer is a danger. He very seldom recognizes his nature or his position. The lecturer is a man who must talk for an hour. France may possibly have acquired the intellectual leadership of Europe when their academic period was cut down to forty minutes. I also have lectured. The lecturer's first problem is to have enough words to fill forty or sixty minutes. The professor is paid for his time, his results are almost impossible to estimate. . . . No teacher has ever failed from ignorance. That is empiric professional knowledge. Teachers fail because they cannot "handle the class." Real education must ultimately be limited to men who INSIST on knowing, the rest is mere sheep-herding.

—Ezra Pound, *ABC of Reading*

or fire:

Let us look at this American artist first. How did he ever get to America, to start with? Why isn't he a European still, like his father before him?

Now listen to me, don't listen to him. He'll tell you the lie you expect. Which is partly your fault for expecting it.

He didn't come in search of freedom of worship. England had more freedom of worship in the year 1700 than America had. Won by Englishmen who wanted freedom and so stopped at home and fought for it. And got it. Freedom of worship? Read the history of New England during the first century of its existence.

Freedom anyhow? The land of the free! This the land of the free! Why, if I say anything that displeases them, the free mob will lynch me, and that's my freedom. Free? Why I have never

been in any country where the individual has such an abject fear
of his fellow countrymen. Because, as I say, they are free to lynch
him the moment he shows he is not one of them. . . .
   All right then, what did they come for? For lots of reasons.
Perhaps least of all in search of freedom of any sort: positive
freedom, that is.

                              —D. H. Lawrence, *Studies in Classic American Literature*

In this last example, Lawrence invests his discourse with even more
urgency by breaking sentences into fragments and what could be
longer paragraphs into snatches of discourse.
   Equally accomplished writers write one long sentence after
another to suggest an inquiring mind exploring an idea:

In any event, up at the front of this March, in the first line, back
of that hollow square of monitors, Mailer and Lowell walked in
this barrage of cameras, helicopters, TV cars, monitors,
loudspeakers, and wavering buckling twisting line of notables,
arms linked (line twisting so much that at times the movement was
in file, one arm locked ahead, one behind, then the line would
undulate about and the other arm would be ahead) speeding up a
few steps, slowing down while a great happiness came back into
the day as if finally one stood under some mythical arch in the
great vault of history, helicopters buzzing about, chop-chop, and
the sense of America divided on this day now liberated some
undiscovered patriotism in Mailer so that he felt a sharp searing
love for his country in this moment and on this day, crossing some
divide in his own mind wider than the Potomac, a love so
lacerated he felt as if a marriage were being torn and children
lost—never does one love so much as then, obviously, then—and
an odor of wood smoke, from where you knew not, was also in
the air, a smoke of dignity and some calm heroism, not unlike the
sense of freedom which also comes when a marriage is
burst—Mailer knew for the first time why men in the front line of
battle are almost always ready to die; there is a promise of some
swift transit. . . .

                              —Norman Mailer, *Armies of the Night*

The sentence goes on for several hundred more words.

Exercise 8-III

First, imitate a passage that has a series of very short sentences. Then imitate the Mailer sentence (you might want to read the rest of it in Book I, Part III, Chapter 4, of *Armies of the Night*). Then try to revise the passages made up of short sentences into just one or two long sentences, in the style of Mailer. Then revise the Mailer passage into a series of short, curt sentences.

METAPHOR, SIMILE, IMAGE

Clarity, vigor, symmetry, rhythm—prose so graced would more than satisfy most of us. And yet, if it offered no virtues other than these, such prose would excite an admiration only for our craft, not for the reach of our invention or imagination. This next passage displays all the stylistic graces we've described so far, but it goes beyond mere craftsmanship. It reveals a truth about pleasure through a figure of speech embedded in a comparison that is itself almost metaphorical.

> The secret of the enjoyment of pleasure is to know when to stop. . . . We do this every time we listen to music. We do not seize hold of a particular chord or phrase and shout at the orchestra to go on playing it for the rest of the evening; on the contrary, however much we may like that particular moment of music, we know that its perpetuation would interrupt and kill the movement of the melody. We understand that the beauty of a symphony is less in these musical moments than in the whole movement from beginning to end. If the symphony tries to go on too long, if at a certain point the composer exhausts his creative ability and tries to carry on just for the sake of filling in the required space of time, then we begin to fidget in our chairs, feeling that he has denied the natural rhythm, has broken the smooth curve from birth to death, and that though a pretense of life is being made, it is in fact a living death.
>
> —Alan W. Watts, *The Meaning of Happiness*

Watts could have written this:

> . . . however much we may like that particular moment of music, we know that its perpetuation would interrupt and spoil the

movement of the melody. . . . we begin to fidget in our chairs, feeling that he has denied the natural rhythm, has interrupted the regular movement from beginning to end, and that though a pretense of wholeness is being made, it is in fact a repeated end.

The two passages are equally clear and graceful. But the first illuminates music—and pleasure—in a way the second does not. The metaphor of birth and the smooth, unbroken curve of life into death startles us with a flash of unexpected truth.

Of metaphor, Aristotle wrote,

By far the greatest thing is to be a master of metaphor. It is the one thing that cannot be learned from others. It is a sign of genius, for a good metaphor implies an intuitive perception of similarity among dissimilars.

A metaphor invites us to see a familiar thing in a new way. Similes do the same, but less intensely, the *like* or *as* moderating the force of the comparison. Compare these:

The schoolmaster is the person who takes the children off the parents' hands for a consideration. That is to say, he establishes a child prison, engages a number of employee schoolmasters as turnkeys, and covers up the essential cruelty and unnaturalness of the situation by torturing the children if they do not learn, and calling this process, which is within the capacity of any fool or blackguard, by the sacred name of Teaching.

—G. B. Shaw, *Sham Education*

. . . he establishes something that is like a child prison, engages a number of employee schoolmasters to act in the way turnkeys do, covers up the essential cruelty and unnaturalness of the situation by doing things to the children that are like torture if they do not learn, and calling this process, which is within the capacity of any fool or blackguard, by the sacred name of Teaching.

Both passages say essentially the same thing about education, but the first with more intensity and immediacy.

You may think that metaphor is appropriate only to poetic writing, or reflective or polemical writing. But metaphor vivifies all kinds of prose. Many historians rely on it:

This is what may be called the common-sense view of history. History consists of a corpus of ascertained facts. The facts are available to the historian in documents, inscriptions, and so on, like fish on the fishmonger's slab. The historian collects them, takes them home, and cooks and serves them in whatever style appeals to him. Acton, whose culinary tastes were austere, wanted them served plain. . . . Sir George Clark, critical as he was of Acton's attitude, himself contrasts the "hard core of facts" in history with the "surrounding pulp of disputable interpretation"—forgetting perhaps that the pulpy part of the fruit is more rewarding than the hard core.

—E. H. Carr, *What Is History?*

So do biologists:

Some of you may have been thinking that, instead of delivering a scientific address, I have been indulging in a flight of fancy. It is a flight, but not of mere fancy, nor is it just an individual indulgence. It is my small personal attempt to share in the flight of the mind into new realms of our cosmic environment. We have evolved wings for such flights, in the shape of the disciplined scientific imagination. Support for those wings is provided by the atmosphere of knowledge created by human science and learning: so far as this supporting atmosphere extends, so far can our wings take us in our exploration.

—Julian Huxley, "New Bottles for Old Wine,"
*Journal of the Royal Anthropological
Institute*

And philosophers:

Suppose I look at the night sky through a piece of heavily smoked glass on which certain lines have been left clear. Then I shall see only the stars that can be made to lie on the lines previously prepared upon the screen, and the stars I do see will be seen as organized by the screen's structure. We can think of a metaphor as such a screen. We can say that the principal subject is "seen through" the metaphorical expression—or, if we prefer, that the principal subject is "projected upon" the field of the subsidiary subject.

—Max Black, "Metaphor," *Models and Metaphors*

And when they are writing of new ideas for which there is yet no standard language, so do physicists:

> Whereas the lepton pair has a positive rest mass when it is regarded as a single particle moving with a velocity equal to the vector sum of the motions of its two components, a photon always has zero rest mass. This difference can be glossed over, however, by treating the lepton pair as the off-spring of the decay of a short-lived photonlike parent called a virtual photon.
> —Leon M. Lederman, "The Upsilon Particle," *Scientific American*

These metaphors serve different ends. Shaw used prison to emphasize a point that he could have made without it, but prisons, turnkeys, and torture invest his argument with an emotional intensity that ordinary language could not communicate. Carr used fish and fruit both to emphasize and to illuminate. He could have expressed his ideas more prosaically, but the literal statement would have been longer and weaker. Black and Lederman used their comparisons not to emphasize, but entirely to explain; neither required any dramatically heightened emphasis.

But if metaphor can sometimes evidence a fresh imagination, it can also betray those of us whose imaginations fall short of its demands. Too often, we use metaphor to gloss over inexact thinking:

> Societies give birth to new values through the differential osmotic flow of daily social interaction. Conflicts evolve when new values collide with the old, a process that frequently spawns yet a new set of values that synthesize the conflict into a reconciliation of opposites.

We get the idea, but through a glass of careless metaphor, and darkly: The birth metaphor suggests a traumatic event, but the new values, it is claimed, result from osmotic flow, a process constituted by a multitude of invisibly small events. Conflicts do not usually "evolve"; they more often occur in an instant, as suggested by the metaphor of collision. The spawning image picks up the metaphor of birth again, but by this time the image is, at best, collectively ludicrous.

Had the writer thought through his ideas carefully, he might have expressed them in clearer, nonfigurative language:

> As we continuously interact with one another in small ways, we gradually create new social values. When one person behaves

according to one of these new values and another according to an
old value, the values may come into conflict, creating a new third
value that reconciles the other two.

Whether even this version would survive the close scrutiny of a social
scientist is open to question. But at least the ideas are accessible to
literal analysis.

Less misleading but more embarrassing are those passages that
confuse extravagance with emphasis. Huxley's passage about the
wings of inquiry flapping in an atmosphere of scientific knowledge
comes close. This next topples over into bathos:

> The slavering maw of inflation is wolfing down the hard-earned
> savings of retired people. As they plummet headlong into the pit
> of penury, they see before them only the prospect of economic
> perdition.

Metaphors also invite trouble if we aren't sensitive to their earlier
incarnations. Many words that we use altogether prosaically
originated in dead metaphors that spring back to life when we least
expect it. We "look over" a problem in order to "handle" it correctly.
Once we "grasp" its difficulty, we can "break" the problem down into
its parts. None of these metaphors is remarkable in any way; indeed,
we are not even conscious of their being metaphors. But when we
conjoin dead metaphors carelessly, we can unwittingly—and often
ludicrously—resurrect their earlier meanings.

> Unless marketing research can get a feel for the tastes of the
> younger buyer, the thrust of any advertising campaign will be
> fruitless.

We can get an idea about tastes, or a feel for preferences; the thrust
of a campaign may be in the wrong direction, or an effort can be
fruitless. But a "feel" for a "taste" is as obscenely silly as a "fruitless
thrust."

Sad to say, there are no simple rules for distinguishing good
metaphors from bad. About the only safe rule is this: If you create a
metaphor that makes you feel good every time you read it, throw it
out. It's sure to be too clever by half. And if you discover yourself
chasing a metaphor through more than two lines, as Huxley did,
start over.

It's tempting to advise struggling writers never to use a metaphor: we can write clearly, persuasively, even movingly without one. But those who seek a prose style that is more than merely clear and concise might keep in mind what Dr. Johnson once said of Jonathan Swift: "The rogue never hazards a metaphor." Swift was one of the great prose craftsmen of English literature, and in fact he ventured a few metaphors. But Johnson was right, too: For all his stylistic wit and brilliance, Swift lacked that flash of imagery and metaphor that makes memorable the prose of some others who could not construct a sentence half so well.

As with a sense of elegance and grace, developing a good ear—or eye—for metaphor takes practice. And perhaps Aristotle was right, too: Perhaps it cannot be learned at all. But the rewards of learning how to handle metaphor go beyond having a style that is merely a bit more mannered than usual. Metaphor is a way of exploring a subject, a way of seeing a subject through a prism of new perspectives.

Of course, a writer just beginning to experiment with metaphor will fail more more often than he will succeed. Almost invariably, whenever we learn a new skill, we exercise its particular virtues to excess: When we first learn to drive, we steer too much; after a course in logic, we attempt to construct every argument out of rigorous syllogisms. And in matters of style, those who master a new device, a new turn of phrase, will use it everywhere. Unfortunately, first attempts at metaphoric elegance are more intrusively obvious and therefore less satisfying than exaggerated efforts toward clarity and simplicity. And so those entirely natural, entirely predictable early failures can discourage and embarrass even the most diligent students of style. I can only reassure those who are chagrined by their infelicities that everyone experiences the same failures, that no one has ever achieved elegant simplicity or effortless elegance without first having failed.

Exercise 8-IV

The following sentences exhibit excessive length, pervasive wordiness, and some unfortunate metaphors. Edit them in whatever ways you think appropriate.

1. I would like to state that the various figures that are contained in the first quarter report that in effect seem to

spell out particular numbers of importance in regard to the facts regarding productivity, particularly the hidden and unseen costs that are clearly a reflection of as yet unseen renewed pressures of an inflationary origin that are throwing a monkey wrench into our research budget, reveal the considerable degree to which we are in special need of research efforts and activities into new and innovative approaches to a way out of the skyrocketing spiral of wages and compensation for labor that is usually classed as unskilled.

2. In order that a solid grasp of the abstract heart of Einstein's theory of relativity be mastered, there is the initial necessity as to seeing the speed of light as a constant factor, regardless of and independent of where the observer rests or what the particular speed of any given observer might perhaps be in relationship to any other object that may be found in the universe, which is an intellectual leap that escapes a great many people.

3. It is certainly the case there should not be the setting of one's sights with too great a reliance in the hope that we are creatures of a rational order who have the capability of molding the emptiness of the vast universe into an element of a deep picture of our relationship to basic and fundamental existence, due to the fact that we are still in possession of many of the animal-type drives that stop us from logical thought processes as to the fact that immortality is not a spoke in the wheel of transient existence.

SUMMING UP: A BIT OF FLAIR

The most obvious traits of a modestly elegant style include both syntactic patterns and a choice of words that raises the passage above the ordinary. But most important, true stylistic elegance demands a quality of thought that makes a reader feel he is confronting a writer of substantial intellectual quality.

I can't tell you how to be a writer of substantial intellectual quality. Nor can I list all the words that would invest your prose with that special distinction. About the best I can do here is list a few of the sentence patterns that you might experiment with when your ideas are equal to a special intention.

1. Balanced, coordinate, and parallel sentence patterns, more often after the subject than before the verb, with members of increasing length.
2. Pauses after each twelve or fifteen words, then a resumption of the sentence.
3. Nominalizations toward the end of a clause, with a sprinkling of prepositional phrases introduced by *of*.
4. Few, if any, sequences of N + N + N . . .
5. A few conventional patterns of usage to signal your audience that you are raising your prose to a level of formality that should command their attention. (See the next lesson.)

Style and Usage

It is not the business of grammar, as some critics seem preposterously to imagine, to give law to the fashions which regulate our speech. On the contrary, from its conformity to these, and from that alone, it derives all its authority and value.

George Campbell

No grammatical rules have sufficient authority to control the firm and established usage of language. Established custom, in speaking and writing, is the standard to which we must at last resort for determining every controverted point in language and style.

Hugh Blair

English usage is sometimes more than mere taste, judgment, and education — sometimes it's sheer luck, like getting across the street.

E. B. White

So far, we've been discussing matters of choice: From among several sentences that might all express the same idea, how do we pick the best one? We might reject

There was an insufficiency of research support.

for

The comptroller did not support our research sufficiently.

But we wouldn't say that the first was grammatically wrong, only less direct and specific than it could be.

At first glance, we might think grammar and usage to be a different matter. When we read in the *American Heritage Dictionary* that *irregardless* is "nonstandard . . . never acceptable" (except when we're trying to be funny), the possibility of our choosing between *irregardless* and *regardless* seems at best academic. *Regardless* versus *irregardless* isn't a matter of better and worse but of right and utterly, irredeemably, wrong.

Now that seems to simplify matters: To choose correctly, we don't need good taste or sound judgment, only a reliable memory. If we remember that *enthuse* is always and everywhere wrong, then *enthuse* does not even rise to the level of conscious decision. We have only to memorize the same kind of prescriptions for a host of other items:

- Don't begin a sentence* with *and* or *but*.
- Don't end a sentence with a preposition*.
- Don't split infinitives*.
- Don't use double negatives.

Unfortunately, questions of usage are not quite that simple: A good many of the rules we find in some dictionaries and in some handbooks of usage have little or no basis in linguistic fact. Other rules of usage are social imperatives that we violate at the risk of seeming at least badly educated. And then there are some rules that we can observe or not, depending on the effect we want.

Now it's important to keep in mind that in this book we're discussing not spoken, but written English. The English-speaking world has a great variety of spoken dialects, each different from the others in its pronunciation, vocabulary, and grammar. Despite what some may think about a "pure Boston English" as opposed to "illiterate Ozark," no local spoken dialect is inherently better—or worse—than the standard dialect spoken in any other part of our country. Every region has a dialect that careful speakers use on those occasions when careful speech is important. And each dialect has its own distinctive features of pronunciation, word choice, and grammar.

But written English is different. For better or worse, we have tacitly agreed on most of the conventions that define careful standard written English in all parts of the English-speaking world. Different parts of the native English-speaking world may spell a few words in different ways: *theatre* versus *theater, gaol* versus *jail, colour* versus *color,* and so on. We may differ on a very few small points of grammar: *I have no money* versus *I don't have any money.* And in different parts of the world, we may have different words for roughly the same things: *dust bin* versus *garbage can, attorney* and *barrister* versus *lawyer, public school* versus *private school,* and so on. But for the most part, native speakers of English write a standard version that is far more uniform than our various local spoken dialects. This development of a written standard apparently occurs in almost every literate society.

rules and *RULES*

To the end of creating this standard written English, grammarians and teachers of English have, over the last four hundred or so years, assembled a variety of prescriptions and proscriptions whose observation, they believe, distinguishes writers who are careful and responsible from those who are not. The rules range from where to put a comma, to how to use *disinterested* and *uninterested,* to the proper case of a pronoun after *is.* But we have hoarded up these rules less on the basis of any intrinsic logical force or on principles of inherent clarity and precision, than on grounds that have been largely idiosyncratic, historically accidental. No universal principle of logic or experience demands that the past tense of *know* be *knew* rather than *knowed,* or that *like* be now and forevermore a preposition, never a conjunction.

As one consequence of this largely random compilation, not all rules of usage have equal standing with all writers of English, even all careful writers of English. A very few especially careful writers and editors have accepted and try to follow every rule. Most careful writers observe fewer, because they have never had all the rules imposed on them by all their editors or teachers, no matter how critical and careful those readers might be in other matters. There are also a few writers who know all the rules, but who also know that not all of them are worth observing, and that other rules are worth observing only on certain occasions.

Whether we choose to be absolutely safe or rhetorically selective depends on both our competence and our confidence. We could adopt the worst case approach: We learn and observe all the rules all the time because somewhere, sometime, someone who believes in one or another of those rules might condemn us for beginning a sentence with *and,* or ending it with a preposition. We keep a stack of grammar books and usage manuals close by to consult as we edit—painfully—every line we write, until we have memorized those rules so thoroughly that we obey them without reflection. But once we do that, we have deprived ourselves of a stylistic flexibility that can be valuable. And sooner or later, we will try to impose all those rules—valid or not—on others. After all, what good is knowing a rule if all we can do is obey it?

But being carefully selective has its problems too, because then we have to learn which rules to ignore and which to observe—and when. And that requires *both* a good memory and sound rhetorical judgment. It also demands the confidence to face up to those who consider a deliberately split infinitive or a singular *data* as a sign of careless writing—or deliberate scorn of careful writing. An attitude short of blind obedience toward every rule in every grammar book need not indicate a bad education or a contemptuous mind: We must reject some of these rules once we recognize how the best writers in fact write—not how they *say* they write, but how they *do* write. If otherwise careful, educated, and intelligent writers of first-rate prose do not avoid ending a sentence with a preposition, then regardless of what some grammarians or editors would say, a preposition at the end of a sentence is not an error of usage.

The standard adopted here is not that of Transcendental Correctness, but of the observable habits of those we could never accuse of having sloppy minds or of deliberately writing careless prose. On the basis of that principle, we can recognize four kinds of "rules." The kinds are simple enough: What's less clear is which rules go in which category.

Real Rules

The first—the most important—category of rules includes those whose violation unequivocally brands you as a writer of nonstandard English. Here are only a few:

1. Double negatives: The engine had *hardly no* systematic care.
2. Incorrect verb forms: They *knowed* that nothing would happen.
3. Double comparatives: This procedure is *more better*.
4. Some adjectives* for adverbs*: They did the work *real good*.
5. Redundant subjects*: *These ideas, they* need explanation.
6. Certain incorrect pronoun forms: *Him* and *me* will study the problem.
7. Some subject-verb disagreements: *They was* ready to begin.

There are others. But they are so egregious that most of you already know that they are almost never violated by educated writers. And because these rules are always observed in even casual writing, their observance passes unremarked: They is rules whose violation we instantly notes, but whose observance we entirely ignore.

Nonrules

A second category of rules includes those whose observance we do not remark, and whose violation we do not remark either. In fact, these are not rules at all, but a species of folklore, widely taught but largely ignored by educated and careful writers everywhere. Now what follows is, perhaps, to a small degree subjective. But it is based on a good deal of time spent reading prose that is carefully written and intended to be carefully read, and I can only assert that the so-called rules listed below are violated so consistently that, unless we indict for bad grammar just about every serious writer of modern

English, we have to reject as misinformed anyone who would try to enforce them.[1]

1. "Never begin a sentence with a coordinating conjunction* such as *and* or *but.*" Allegedly, not this:

> *But,* it will be asked, is tact not an individual gift, therefore highly variable in its choices? *And* if that is so, what guidance can a manual offer, other than that of its author's prejudices—mere impressionism?
>
> —Wilson Follett, *Modern American Usage: A Guide,* edited and completed by Jacques Barzun et al.

2. "Never begin a sentence with *because.*" Allegedly, not this:

> *Because* we have access to so much historical fact, today we know a good deal about changes within the humanities which were not apparent to those in any age much before our own and which the individual scholar must constantly reflect on.
>
> —Walter Ong, S.J., "The Expanding Humanities and the Individual Scholar," *PMLA*

but presumably, this:

> *Since* we have access to so much historical fact, today we. . . .

or

> We have access to much historical fact. *Consequently* today we. . . .

This proscription appears in no handbook of usage I know of, but the belief seems to have a popular currency among many students. It must stem from advice intended to avoid sentence fragments such as this:

> The application was rejected. *Because the deadline had passed.*

When the *because*-clause that opens a sentence is followed by a main clause, and punctuated so that the two constitute a single punctuated sentence, then it is entirely correct:

> *Because* the deadline had passed, the application was rejected.

---

[1] Each citation offered as an example of a "rule" violated is in its original form, except for the italics, which I have added.

3. "When referring to an inanimate referent, use the relative pronoun *that*—not *which*—for restrictive* clauses; use *which* for nonrestrictive clauses." Allegedly not this:

> Next is a typical situation *which* a practiced writer corrects "for style" virtually by reflex action.
> —Jacques Barzun, *Simple and Direct*

but presumably, this:

> Next is a typical situation *that* a practiced writer corrects "for style" virtually by reflex action.

Both are entirely correct.

4. "Use *each other* to refer to two, *one another* to refer to three or more." Allegedly, not this:

Now "society" is ever in search of novelty,—and it is a limited body of well-to-do women and men of leisure. From the almost exclusive association of these persons with *each other,* there arises a kind of special vocabulary, which is constantly changing. . . .
> —James B. Greenough and George L. Kittredge, *Words and Their Ways in English Speech*

but presumably, this:

> From the almost exclusive association of these persons with *one another,* there arises a kind of special vocabulary. . . .

One another may be just a shade more formal than *each other,* but neither phrase is, in good usage, limited in the way the rule states.

5. "Use *between* with two, *among* with three or more." Allegedly, not this:

> . . . government remained in the hands of fools and adventurers, foreigners and fanatics, who *between* them went near to wrecking the work of the Tudor monarchy. . . .
> —Geo. Macaulay Trevelyan, *A Shortened History of England*

but presumably, this:

> . . . government remained in the hands of fools and adventurers, foreigners and fanatics, who *among* them went near to wrecking the work of the Tudor monarchy. . . .

Among goes with three or more, of course, but *between* also occurs in that context.

6. "Don't use *which* or *this* to refer to a whole clause." Allegedly, not this:

> Although the publishers have not yet destroyed the plates of the second edition of Merriam-Webster's unabridged dictionary, they do not plan to keep it in print, which is a pity.
> —Dwight McDonald, "The String Untuned," *The New Yorker*

but presumably, this:

> Although the publishers have not yet destroyed the plates of . . . they do not plan to keep it in print, a decision which is a pity.

Occasionally, this kind of construction can be ambiguous. In the next example, does the letter make her happy, or the fact that it was given to her?

> We gave her the letter, which made her happy.

Here, a summative modifier makes the meaning unambiguous:

> We gave her the letter, *a thoughtful act* that made her happy.

When it is clear what the *which* refers to, this kind of general *which* is entirely appropriate.

7. "Use *fewer* with nouns you can count, *less* with quantities you cannot." Allegedly, not this:

> I can remember no *less than five occasions* when the correspondence columns of The Times rocked with volleys of letters from the

academic profession protesting that academic freedom is in danger and the future of scholarship threatened.

> —Noel Gilroy Annan. Lord Annan, "The Life of the Mind in British Universities Today," *ACLS Newsletter*

but presumably, this:

> I can remember no *fewer than five occasions* when. . . .

It is true that *fewer* is restricted to countable nouns. But *less* now frequently occurs with countable nouns in the prose of many who certainly qualify as careful writers.

8. "Use *due to,* meaning 'because of,' only to introduce a phrase modifying a noun, never to introduce a phrase that modifies a verb." Allegedly, not this:

> . . . cooperation between the Department of Economics and the Business School and between the Business School and the Law School will be much greater ten years from now than at present, *due to* the personal relations of the younger men on the three faculties.

> —James Bryant Conant, The *President's Report: 1951–1952,* Harvard University Press

but presumably, this:

> . . . cooperation will be much greater ten years from now than at present, *because of* the personal relations of the younger men on the three faculties.

There are also a few individual words whose usage is sometimes proscribed by extremely conservative teachers and editors. But the actual usage of these words by careful writers is, as a rule, unremarked by equally careful readers. Most careful writers use *since* with the meaning of "because"; *alternative* to refer to one of three or more choices; *anticipate* to mean "expect"; *continuous* for *continual* and vice versa; *contact* as a general verb meaning "communicate with." Though *data* and *media* as singulars are *bêtes noires* for some observers, they are used as singular nouns by large numbers of careful writers in the same way they use *agenda* and *insignia. (Strata, errata,* and *criteria* still seem to be plurals for most careful writers.) *Infer* for *imply* and *disinterested* for *uninterested* are countenanced by some standard dictionaries whose editors base their decisions about acceptability on the usage of careful writers. Many teachers and editors strongly disagree.

In the most formal of circumstances, circumstances in which you would want to avoid the slightest hint of violating even the most trivial point of usage, you might decide to observe these rules (excepting 1 and 2). In most ordinary circumstances, though, they are ignored by most careful writers. If you decide to adopt the worst-case approach and observe them all, all the time—well, to each his own. Private virtues are their own reward.

Optional Rules

These next rules complement the first group: For the most part, few readers will notice if you violate them. But when you observe them, you will signal a level of formality that few careful readers will miss.

1. "Never split an infinitive." Some purists would demand this:

> . . . one wonders why Dr. Gove and his editors did not think of labelling *knowed* as substandard right where it occurs, and one suspects that they wanted *to conceal the fact slightly* or at any rate to put off its exposure as long as decently possible.

But Dwight McDonald, a linguistic archconservative, wrote this:

> . . . one wonders why Dr. Gove and his editors did not think of labelling *knowed* as substandard right where it occurs, and one suspects that they wanted *to slightly conceal* the fact or at any rate to put off its exposure as long as decently possible.
> —Dwight McDonald, "The String Untuned," *The New Yorker*

The split infinitive is now so common among the very best writers that when we make an effort to avoid splitting it, we invite notice, whether we intend to or not.

2. "Use *shall* as the first person simple future, *will* for second and third person simple future; use *will* to mean strong

intention in the first person, *shall* for second and third person." Some purists would demand this:

I *shall* end with two remarks by two wise old women of the civilized eighteenth century.

But F. L. Lucas wrote this:

I *will* end with two remarks by two wise old women of the civilized eighteenth century.

—F. L. Lucas, "What Is Style?" *Holiday*

3. "Always use *whom* as the object of a verb or preposition." Purists would demand this:

Soon after you confront this matter of preserving your identity, another question will occur to you: "For *whom* am I writing?"

But William Zinsser wrote this:

Soon after you confront this matter of preserving your identity, another question will occur to you: "*Who* am I writing for?"

—William Zinsser, *On Writing Well*

Whom is a small but distinct flag of conscious correctness, especially when the *whom* is in fact wrong:

We found a candidate *whom* we thought was most qualified.

The rule: The form of the pronoun depends on whether it is a subject or an object of its own clause. Since *who* is the subject of *was* in

We found a candidate 🠕 we thought *who* was most qualified.

who is the correct form, not *whom*. In this next example, *whom* is the object of *overlooked*:

We found a candidate 🠕 we thought we had overlooked *whom*

If you are in doubt about the matter, try dropping the *who/whom* altogether:

> We found a candidate we thought we had overlooked.

4. "Never end a sentence with a preposition." Purists, presumably, would demand this:

> The peculiarities of legal English are often used as a stick *with which* to beat the official.

But Sir Ernest Gowers wrote this:

> The peculiarities of legal English are often used as a stick to beat the official *with*.
>
> —Sir Ernest Gowers, *The Complete Plain Words*

The first is more formal than the second, but the second is still grammatically correct. In fact, whenever we move a preposition before its object, we make the sentence a bit more formal. And any obligatory *whom* after the preposition only compounds the formality. Compare:

> The man *with whom* I spoke was not the man *to whom* I had been referred.

> The man I spoke *with* was not the man I had been referred *to*.

5. "Do not use *whose* as the possessive pronoun for an inanimate referent." Purists would demand this:

> And, on other occasions, the meaning comes from other partly parallel uses, the relevance *of which* we can feel, without necessarily being able to state it explicitly.

But I. A. Richards wrote this:

> And on other occasions, the meaning comes from other partly parallel uses, *whose* relevance we can feel, without necessarily being able to state it explicitly.
>
> —I. A. Richards, *The Philosophy of Rhetoric*

6. "Use *one* as a generalized pronoun instead of *you*." Purists, presumably, would demand this:

When explicit meanings are wrongly combined, *one* gets a logical fault (this is oversimplifying somewhat, but *one* may take it as a first approximation).

But Monroe Beardsley wrote this:

When explicit meanings are wrongly combined, *you* get a logical fault (this is oversimplifying somewhat, but *take* it as a first approximation).

—Monroe C. Beardsley, "Style and Good Style," *Reflections on High School English: NDEA Institute Lectures*, ed. Gary Tate

7. "Do not refer to *one* with *he* or *his;* repeat *one*." Purists would demand this:

Thus, unless *one* belongs to that tiny minority who can speak directly and beautifully, *one* should not write as *one* talks.

But Theodore Bernstein wrote this:

Thus, unless one belongs to that tiny minority who can speak directly and beautifully, *one* should not write as *he* talks.

—Theodore M. Bernstein, *The Careful Writer*

8. "When expressing a contrary-to-fact statement, use the subjunctive form of the verb, and for *be* use *were*." Purists would demand this:

Another suffix that is not a living one, but is sometimes treated as if it *were,* is -*al;* it will serve to illustrate a special point.

H. W. Fowler wrote this:

Another suffix that is not a living one, but is sometimes treated as if it *was,* is -*al;* &. . . .

—H. W. Fowler, *A Dictionary of Modern English Usage*

As the English subjunctive quietly fades into linguistic history, it leaves a residue of forms infrequent enough to impart to a sentence a slightly archaic—and therefore formal—tone. We regularly use the simple past tense to express most subjunctives:

> If we *knew* what to do, we *would* do it.

Be is the problem: Strictly construed, the subjunctive demands *were,* but *was* is gradually replacing it:

> If this *were* 1941, a loaf of bread would cost twenty cents.

> If this *was* 1941, a loaf of bread would cost twenty cents.

A FINE POINT: Special Formality

The list of items that create a special sense of formality might include a few others that don't involve disputed points of usage, but do let you raise a passage to a style a bit above the ordinary.

1. Negative inversion. When we invert, we reverse the normal order. Probably the most famous negative inversion is President John F. Kennedy's

   > *Ask not* what your country can do for you, but what you can do for your country.

Negatives such as *rarely, never, not, only,* and so on, typically let you put a verb before its subject:

> *Never have* so many owed so much to so few.

> *Rarely do* we confront a situation such as this.

> *Only once has* this corporation failed to pay a dividend.

2. Conditional inversion. Instead of beginning a conditional clause with *if,* begin it with *should, were,* or *had:*

   > *If* anyone should question the grounds on which this decision was made, we can point to centuries of tradition.

   > *Should* anyone question the grounds on which this decision was made, we can point to centuries of tradition.

If there had been any objections, they would have been met.

Had there been any objections, they would have been met.

If I were prepared to answer you now, I should do so happily.

Were I prepared to answer you now, I should do so happily.

3. Instead of *do not have to,* use *need not:*

You *don't have to* answer now.

You *need not* answer now.

4. Instead of *does not have,* use *have no:*

The court *does not have* any precedent to follow.

The court *has no* precedent to follow.

Bêtes Noires

Now, there is a category of usages that for some teachers and editors have become objects of special abuse. Why such special feeling should be invested in these particular items is difficult to explain: It may simply be that they have become the symbolic flags around which some of those most intensely concerned with linguistic purity (whatever that may be) have tacitly agreed to rally. None of these items interferes with clarity and concision; indeed, some of them let us save a word here and there. But for one reason or another, they arouse such intense feeling in so many editors, teachers, and ordinary citizens that you should be aware of their special status.

1. *Like* for *as* or *as if.* Not this:

These operations failed *like* the earlier ones did.

It appears *like* we require further data on this matter.

But this:

These operations failed *as* the earlier ones did.

It appears *as if* we require further data on this matter.

2. *From* after *different,* not *than* or *to.* Not this:

   These numbers are *different than* the ones you gave me earlier.

   We must approach this problem *differently than* we did last year.

But this:

   These numbers are *different from* the ones you gave me earlier.

   We must approach this problem *differently from the way* we did last year.

3. *Hopefully,* only when the subject of the clause can be hopeful. Not this:

   Hopefully, the matter will be resolved soon.

But this:

   I hopefully say that the matter will be resolved soon.

4. *Unique* qualified with a *very, rather, quite, somewhat,* etc. Never this:

   A *very unique* product was developed by his company.

5. *Finalize* used to mean *finish, complete, end.*

6. *Irregardless* instead of *regardless.*

And a Special Problem: Pronouns and Sexism

We expect verbs to agree with their subjects. Not this:

   There *is* several *reasons* for this.

but this:

   There *are* several *reasons* for this.

So do we ordinarily expect pronouns to agree in number with what they refer to. Not this:

   The early *efforts* to oppose the building of a hydrogen bomb failed because *it* was not coordinated with the scientific and political communities. *No one* was willing to step forth and expose *themselves* to the anti-Communist hysteria unless *they* had the backing of others.

but this:

The early *efforts* to oppose the building of a hydrogen bomb failed because *they* were not coordinated with the scientific and political communities. *No one* was willing to step forth and expose *himself* to the anti-Communist hysteria unless *he* had the backing of others.

There are two problems here: The first is which pronoun to use when you refer to a singular noun that is plural in meaning: *group, committee, staff, administration* and so on. Some editors and teachers use a singular pronoun when the group acts as a single entity:

The *committee* has reviewed the applications but has not yet made *its* decision.

But when the members of the group act individually, some writers use a plural pronoun:

The *committee* received the application, but not all of *them* have read it.

It is probably just as common these days to find the plural used in both senses.

The second problem is what pronoun to use to refer to singular indefinite pronouns such as *everyone, everybody, someone, somebody,* and to indefinite singular nouns that refer to people but not to their gender: *a teacher, a person, a student,* and so on. In less formal writing, the plural *they* is being used more and more to refer to singular referents:

Everyone who spends four years in college realizes what a soft life *they* had only when *they* get a nine-to-five job, with no summer and Christmas vacations.

When *a person* gets involved with drugs, no one can help *them* unless *they* want to help *themselves.*

In both cases, more formal usage requires the singular pronoun:

> *Everyone* who spends four years in college realizes what a soft life *he* had only when *he* gets a nine-to-five job, with no summer and Christmas vacations.

> When *a person* gets involved with drugs, no one can help *him* unless *he* wants to help *himself.*

But when we observe the rule, we raise another, thornier, problem—the matter of sexist language.

Obviously, what we perceive to be our social responsibilities and the sensitivities of our audience must always come first: Many believe that we lose little, and perhaps gain much, by substituting *humanity* for *mankind, police officer* for *policeman, synthetic* for *man-made*, etc. (Those who ask whether we should also substitute *personhole cover* for *manhole cover*, or *person-in-the moon* for *man-in-the-moon,* either miss the point, or are trying to make a contentious one.) And if we are writing for an audience that might judge our language sexist, then sheer common sense demands that we find ways to express our ideas in nonsexist ways, even at the cost of a little wordiness. Little harm is done when we substitute for *The Dawn of Man* something like *The Dawn of Human Society.*

But a generic *he* is different: If we reject *he* as a generic pronoun because it is sexist, and *they* as a generic singular pronoun because it is diffuse or potentially ambiguous (its formal "grammaticality" aside), we are left with either a clumsily intrusive *he or she,* or an imperative to rewrite sentence after sentence in arbitrary and sometimes awkward ways.

Now, no one with even the slightest ear for style can choose the first alternative without flinching:

> When a writer does not consider the ethnicity of his or her readers, they may respond in ways he or she would not have anticipated to certain words that for him or her are entirely innocent of ethnic bias.

So we have to rewrite. We can begin by substituting something for the singular *his:*

> When a writer does not consider the ethnicity of his readers . . .

> When a writer does not consider the reader's ethnicity . . .

We can also try passives, nominalizations, and other phrases that let us drop pronouns serving as subjects and objects:

> The *failure to consider* a reader's ethnic background may result in an *unexpected response* to certain words that may seem to the writer to be entirely innocent of ethnic bias.

And when it's appropriate, we can always trying switching the pronoun from a third person *he* to a second person *you* or a first person *we:*

> If *we* do not consider the ethnic background of *our* readers, *they* may respond in ways *we* would not expect to certain words that may seem to *us* to be entirely innocent of ethnic bias.

Finally, each of us has to decide whether the social consequences of a sexist *he* justify the effort required to avoid it and the occasionally graceless or even diffuse style that can result. No one committed to writing the clearest, the most fluent and precise prose can fail to recognize the value of a generic *he:* It lets us begin a sentence briskly and smoothly; it lets us assign to a verb specific agency; it lets us avoid ambiguity, diffuseness, and abstraction. But for the kind of practical writing that most of us do, day in and day out, those fine nuances of phrasing and cadence may be less important than the social objective of an unqualified nonsexist language. If its cost is but a few moments' thought and an occasionally strained sentence, the choice would seem self-evident.

precision and *PRECISION*

Now, different readers might assign some of the items taken up in this lesson to categories different from those that I have suggested. Some would add many other points of usage. And some would insist that every one of these items, and many more besides, belong in that first category, those constructions that invariably distinguish speakers and writers of standard English from those who are not. If we don't respect them all, they argue, we begin the slide down the slippery slope to inarticulateness.

The urge to regulate—and by regulating, fix—language has a long tradition, not only in the English-speaking world, but in literate cultures everywhere. We invest a great deal of ourselves first in learning our forms of speech, and then in mastering the fine points that, we are told, distinguish careful, responsible English from the language of those who are crude, careless, and unreliable. Perhaps we believe that both our language and our values are threatened when we hear others use different forms, especially when those others seem to have interests and values that threaten ours.

We usually express our linguistic values as a passionate concern for "precision," for maintaining "standards." Unless we maintain those standards, some of us argue, our language will degenerate into a barbarousness unequal to the needs of cultured intercourse. But since no language has ever been known to "degenerate" into a form that defeats effective communication, it is unlikely ours ever will, regardless of our attitude toward these few items of usage.

We can put the matter of precision more usefully like this: If we ignore imprecise and clumsy writing, people will go on writing clumsily and imprecisely—in all the ways we've spent eight lessons discussing. And if they go on writing clumsily and imprecisely, then eventually clumsiness and imprecision will become the accepted standard of written discourse. And when that happens, clumsy and imprecise thinking cannot be far behind. *That* is a matter worth some passion.

The trouble begins when we try to define the object of our passion, for, of course, we need examples of imprecise and clumsy writing that we can hold up for deserved public scorn. But not many of us are going to memorize for this purpose good examples of bad writing (and even if we did, they would have no general use: Who writes the same sentence twice?). We find it much easier to assemble a list of stock items that we can cite as reliable examples of careless writing. When those items have been steadily abused for two and a half centuries, they become not just random items of disputed usage, but symbols of the careful writer's dedication to the quality of his product. That's why, on TV talk shows and in newspapers and magazines, critics who deplore the declining state of the language always rehearse the same stock errors: *like* for *as, different than* for *different from, disinterested* for *uninterested, finalize, hopefully,* etc. These items have become the instantly recognized symbols of what we say we are fighting against in our determination to defend the precision of our language. In fact, if tomorrow every writer of English began to observe every one of these rules of usage, we should have to invent new ones, for their universal observation would substantially improve the langauge not at all and would bereave of their stock examples those for whom the purity of English has become a special passion.

All of us who are committed to excellence in prose share a common end: a style that communicates effectively, even elegantly. And that, by and large, is a style that is clear, precise, and economical. Some believe that we shall achieve that end only if we include in our definition of precision a precise adherence to all these rules of usage. Others do not. Wherever you decide to take your stand, keep this in mind: A writer who faithfully observes every one of these rules can still write wretched prose. And some of the most lucid, precise, and educated prose is written by those for whom *some* of these rules have no force whatsoever.

SUMMING UP: LISTS ARE NOT SYSTEMS

Because usage is idiosyncratic, individual, unpredictable, I can't offer any broad generalizations, any useful principles, by which to decide any given item. Indeed, if usage did submit to logical consideration, it would be no issue, for most "errors" of usage result when we extend a generalization too far: *Knowed* results when a speaker applies a past tense rule once too often. Finally, I think, we choose among these items less on the basis of their real or supposed usage than according to a sense of our own personal style. Some of us are straightforward, plain, direct; others take pleasure in a bit of elegance, a touch of self-conscious "class." The *shalls* and the *wills,* the *whos* and the *whoms,* the split and the unsplit infinitives are the small choices that let us express a sense of our individual personae.

Lesson Ten

Style and Punctuation

I know there are some Persons who affect to despise it, and treat this whole Subject with the utmost Contempt, as a Trifle far below their Notice, and a Formality unworthy of their Regard: They do not hold it difficult, but despicable; and neglect it, as being above it.

Yet many learned Men have been highly sensible to its Use; and some ingenious and elegant Writers have condescended to point their Works with Care; and very eminent Scholars have not disdained to teach the Method of doing it with Propriety.

James Burrow

There is much more difficulty in pointing, than people are generally aware of. —In effect, there is scarce any thing in the province of the grammarians so little fixed and ascertained as this. The rules usually laid down are impertinent, dark, and deficient; and the practice, at present, perfectly capricious, authors varying not only from one another, but from themselves, too....

Ephraim Chambers

There are some punctuations that are interesting and there are some that are not.

Gertrude Stein

For most of us, punctuation is a housekeeping problem: We engage it only long enough to keep things straight. And yet, deployed carefully and sensitively, commas, colons, and semicolons can make our sentences* not only clear but even a bit elegant. Good punctuation won't turn a stylistic monotone into the Hallelujah Chorus, but a little knowledge and a bit of care can produce very satisfying results.

Each section of this chapter begins with the least you have to know about punctuation and then explores some of its niceties. We'll address the matter as a functional problem: How do we punctuate the beginning, the middle, and the end of a sentence? And since how we punctuate the end of a sentence most visibly comments on our basic literacy, we'll begin there.

PUNCTUATING ENDS

In Lesson 4, we distinguished two kinds of sentences: *punctuated** and *grammatical**. A *punctuated sentence* is whatever begins with a capital letter and ends with a period, question mark, or exclamation point. A *grammatical sentence* is the least that we can stop with one of those marks with nothing left over. The least a sentence can have is a verb* that signals past or present. And except for imperative sentences *(Stop that!)*, a grammatical sentence always provides that verb with a subject*. Together, the subject and verb constitute the heart of a clause*.

A clause is *independent** if it does not grammatically attach to, depend on, function as, a part of any other clause. You can punctuate an independent clause as a separate sentence:

> From 1925 to 1975, common stocks averaged an 8.5 percent return.

A *dependent* or *subordinate clause* usually begins with a word that signals its dependency: *because, although, if, since, when, though, after, before, as, which, who, whom, whose, that, whether.* We usually don't punctuate a dependent clause as a separate sentence. Not this:

> *Because* from 1925 to 1975, common stocks averaged an 8.5 percent return.

Which from 1925 to 1975 averaged an 8.5 percent return.

That from 1925 to 1975 common stocks averaged an 8.5 percent return.

Invariably, such a clause will attach to an independent clause that precedes or follows it:

Common stocks would have been a good investment over the last half *century, because* from 1925 to 1975 they averaged an 8.5 percent return.

You would have been wise to invest in common *stocks, which* from 1925 to 1975 averaged an 8.5 percent return.

Few people are aware of this *fact, that* from 1925 to 1975 common stocks averaged an 8.5 percent return.

Another common kind of fragment begins with *-ing:*

Stocks have been a good investment. *Averaging* an 8.5 percent return from 1925 to 1975.

The phrase beginning with *averaging* has no subject, and *averaging* is not a form of a verb that could signal past or present. It would need an *are* or *were:*

Stocks *were* averaging an 8.5 percent return from 1925 to 1975.

If we do not provide *averaging* with a subject and a finite* verb, then we have to attach it to what goes before:

Stocks have been a good *investment, averaging* an 8.5 percent. . . .

Whenever you reach the end of a grammatical sentence, including whatever dependent clauses are part of it, you can stop with a period. But you can stop less emphatically in a few other ways: First, you can use a semicolon to indicate that the clause that follows the semicolon is closely linked to the clause before it:

In 1957 and again in 1960, Congress passed civil rights laws that remedied problems of registration and *voting; both* had significant political consequences throughout the South.

The Beatniks were the first identifiable postwar group to reject the values of the *middle-class; subsequent* years gave us Hippies, Yippies, flower children, dropouts, communards, and Weathermen.

You can end one independent clause with a comma if the next clause is a grammatical sentence and you begin it with *and, but, yet, for, so, or,* or *nor:*

In the 1950s religion came to be viewed as a bulwark against *communism, so it* was not long after that that atheism was felt to be a threat to national security.

American intellectuals have always followed the lead of European Marxist *philosophy, but American* academic culture has proven to be an inhospitable environment for the flourishing of communistic ideas.

It is, of course, always considered absolutely wrong to run one independent clause onto the next with no connective at all:

The stock market is finally beginning *to recover it was* depressed for several years.

SOME FINE POINTS: Special Kinds of Closeness

If two sentences are relatively short, closely linked, and balanced, you can link two grammatical sentences, two independent clauses, with just a comma (Be sure that neither has any internal commas.):

Football appeals to our love for violent *collision, baseball* satisfies our more measured and graceful tastes.

Women have always been *underpaid, they* are only now beginning to do something about it.

Though it is not difficult to find sentences punctuated this way in the best prose, many teachers consider this kind of punctuation incorrect, so it is wise to have a sense of your audience before you experiment.

Nor is it uncommon for writers to join two short clauses with the conjunction alone, omitting the comma:

> Oscar Wilde brazenly violated one of the fundamental laws of British *society and we* all know what happened to him.

These four ways of linking clauses—semicolon, comma + coordinating conjunction, comma alone, and conjunction alone—create an increasingly tight bond between the ideas those clauses express, so it is important that the ideas in fact be balanced.

A mark of punctuation that lets you be just the slightest bit elegant is the colon: It is formal shorthand for *to illustrate, for example, for instance, that is, let me expand on what I just said, therefore, the conclusion is obvious:*

> Only one question remains to be answered: Who assumes responsibility if the project loses money?

> Dance is not one of our more widely supported art forms: Not one dance company can count on operating in the black every year, and outside of two or three major cities, we find hardly any active companies.

> Computer operators are fond of comparing their hardware to the human brain: They wax eloquent on its speed, its resourcefulness, its flexibility.

A colon also lets you balance one clause against another a bit more elegantly than a comma or semicolon:

> Civil disobedience is the public conscience of a democracy: Mass enthusiasm is the public consensus of a tyranny.

A dash can serve as a somewhat less formal colon—it has a kind of casual immediacy that suggests not quite a tacked-on afterthought, but not the formal presentation of a colon, either:

> Stonehenge is one of the wonders of the ancient world—only a genius could have conceived, planned, and executed its mathematical and astronomical perfection.

(Try that with a colon—you'll sense the difference.)

You can choose to capitalize or not the first word in a clause following a colon: A capital letter makes what follows a bit more prominent and emphatic. Ordinarily, we don't capitalize what follows a dash.

Avoid breaking a clause with a colon between a verb or preposition and a long object. Not this:

> Effective genetic counseling *requires: a thorough* knowledge of statistical genetics, an awareness of medical choices open to prospective parents, psychological competence to deal with emotional trauma.

Complete the clause before you begin a substantial list:

> Effective genetic counseling requires the following *preparation: a thorough knowledge* of statistical genetics, an awareness of. . . .

PUNCTUATING BEGINNINGS

If you begin a sentence directly with a subject, you have no immediate problems. Problems begin when you introduce a sentence with modifying words, phrases, and clauses. You can follow a few absolute rules, but more often you have to exercise good judgment.

The (almost) Absolute Rules

1. Never put a comma after an introductory subordinating conjunction such as *because, if, although, while, since, as, before, after.* Not this:

   Because, inflation is increasing faster than interest rates, people are investing their money in art objects.

2. Resist a comma after the introductory coordinating conjunctions *and, but, yet, for, so, or, nor.* Not this:

   But, we cannot know whether life on other planets realizes that we're here and simply prefers to ignore us.

   And, this conclusion supports that of earlier research.

Some writers who punctuate heavily will put a comma after *and, but, yet, for, so, or, nor* if an introductory word or phrase follows:

> *Yet, during this period, prices* continued to rise.

That is a matter of taste.

3. Generally put a comma after introductory words or phrases such as *however, nevertheless, regardless, instead, on the other hand, as a result, consequently, moreover, furthermore, that is, also, fortunately, obviously, allegedly, incidentally*—any word or phrase that comments on the whole of the following sentence:

> *Furthermore, psychological* studies indicate that student radicals are no more neurotic or disturbed than others.

If you find yourself introducing sentence after sentence with words like these, you might consider revising a bit. A comma after just a word or two slows the pace of a sentence just when it should be gaining momentum. Too many such sentences retard the flow of a whole section.

Four introductory words often appear without a following comma: *now, therefore, thus, hence:*

> *Now it* is clear that many constituencies will not support this position.

> *Thus the* only alternative is to choose some other action.

4. Always separate an introductory word, phrase, or clause—no matter how short—from what follows if a reader might misunderstand:

> When the lawyer concludes the opening statement from the floor may begin.

> In most cases we have treated these conditions over a period of several years.

If you open a sentence with a short introductory phrase before a short subject, you don't need a comma:

> *Once again* we find similar responses to exodermal stimuli.

In 1945 few returning servicemen anticipated the dramatic social changes that had transformed American society.

In many areas of the country gasoline prices have risen twice as fast as food prices.

It's not an error of usage to put a comma there, but modern writers tend to use less punctuation than even those of the recent past.

SOME FINE POINTS: Close Connections

With introductory subordinate clauses, there are some other considerations: How closely does the meaning of the introductory clause relate to the meaning of the main clause? If you open with a subordinate clause whose subject is the same as the subject of the main clause, and the meaning of one clause closely depends on the meaning of the other, you probably won't need a comma:

When Hitler realized his Eastern front had collapsed he resolved to destroy every city through which his army would retreat.

But if the subjects of the two clauses differ and the ideas contrast, then you probably do need a comma. Compare:

Because we have accepted the interpretation of the *IRS we* will drop all further appeals.

Although the IRS has overruled this *interpretation, we* will continue to follow our original procedures.

Semicolons have no use between an introductory element and a subject, so you can forget about them there. But if your subject is a long list, then a colon or a dash followed by a summative subject can be useful. Compare

The President, the Vice-President, the Secretaries of the Executive Departments, the Supreme Court Justices, Senators, and members of the House of Representatives take an oath of office that pledges them to uphold the Constitution.

The President, the Vice-President, the Secretaries of the Executive Departments, the Supreme Court Justices, Senators, and members of the House of *Representatives: all of them* take an oath of office that pledges them to uphold the Constitution.

Drugs, gambling, violence, poverty, disease, despair constitute a familiar list of afflictions that can destroy the fabric of a community.

Drugs, gambling, violence, poverty, disease, *despair—they* constitute a familiar list of afflictions that can destroy the fabric of a community.

You can get the effect of a short subject with a word that sums up the longer series of items. Whether you choose the dash or the colon depends mostly on how formal you want to be.

PUNCTUATING THE MIDDLE

Explaining how to punctuate inside a sentence, clause, or phrase is messy, because we have to consider combinations of grammar, meaning, and rhythm. There are, though, three principles that you can keep in mind:

1. Set off with commas or dashes that which distinctly interrupts.
2. Set off with commas, dashes, or parentheses that which loosely comments on or explains essential parts of a clause or phrase.
3. Set off with commas or semicolons items in a series of three or more.

Interruptions

We've discussed these before. When you insert any kind of phrase or clause between a subject and its verb, you usually have to set off that interruption with commas:

Religious *education, I repeat,* is an affair of the private conscience, not of the body politic.

The history of every animal *species, regardless of its evolutionary status, proves* that the most adaptive survive the longest.

This one principle of TV *programming, because it simply overpowers all other considerations, determines* what each of us will watch morning, noon, and night.

(Better yet—avoid the interruptions. Move the interrupter.)
Adverbs* or phrases inside a verb phrase* take commas or not, depending on what our ear prefers:

Twentieth-century poetry *has in recent years become* more comprehensible to the average reader.

Twentieth-century poetry *has, in recent years, become* more comprehensible to the average reader.

It depends entirely on how emphatic we want to be.

If you separate a verb and its object with a phrase or word that is shorter than the object, you don't have to set it off with commas:

In moments of great anxiety, we *see perhaps too clearly the stuff* of which our characters are made.

But if the object is considerably shorter and you want to arrange the words for the greatest impact, you might set off the interruption with a comma:

The antagonisms between the scientific and humanistic communities have *created, in virtually every quarter of the scholarly and intellectual world, utter* distrust.

Loose Commentary

What counts as "loose commentary" depends on meaning, not on grammar. The usual distinction is between *restrictive** and *nonrestrictive** modifiers. A nonrestrictive modifier is "loose"; it adds information to describe something that has already been identified sufficiently. Compare these:

It was necessary partly to reconstruct the larynx, *which had received a traumatic injury,* by means of cartilage obtained from the shoulder.

Tax deduction dependency is awarded to the *parent with whom the child principally resides.*

Since we have only one larynx, merely naming it identifies it sufficiently. Anything more we say about it is loose, *nonrestrictive, nonspecifying* commentary, and so we set it off with commas. But since children have two parents, simply referring to one of them as *parent* doesn't identify which parent we mean. So to *parent* we add a *restrictive,* specifying modifier to completely identify *which* parent we mean. And in that case, we *don't* set off the modifier with commas. This can get fairly delicate when we deal with phrases:

> The process was repeated a fourth time successfully.

> The process was repeated a fourth time, successfully.

In the first, each of the repetitions was successful; in the second, we can be sure only that the fourth repetition was successful.

Phrases and clauses that conclude a sentence often call for a comma unless they are essential to the meaning of the main clause. Compare these:

> Hemingway wandered *through Europe, seeking some environment* where he could write what he felt he had to.

> Hemingway spent *most of his time seeking some environment* where he could write what he felt he had to.

> All offices will be closed from July 2 *through July 6, as announced* in the daily bulletin.

> When closing the offices, it is important *to secure all desks and safes as prescribed* in Operating Manual 45-23a.

> Those who describe what a technologically splendid future we have to look forward to usually underestimate the effect of seemingly minor *social changes, at least insofar as* this country is concerned.

> These records must *be maintained at least until the IRS* has decided whether to review them.

But again, this is often settled by a good ear rather than a fixed rule.

In most of these cases, a dash rather than a comma would be more casual—or striking:

> The process was repeated a fourth *time—successfully.*

It was necessary to fix up his voice *box—which* really got hit hard—by taking some cartilage from his shoulder.

A dash is particularly useful when the chunk of "loose commentary" is itself broken up with commas. This is just a bit confusing:

All the nations of Central Europe, Poland, Czechoslovakia, Hungary, Roumania, Bulgaria, and Yugoslavia, have known what it is like to be in the middle of an East-West tug-of-war.

But if we set off that middle chunk with dashes, the sentence is much clearer:

All the nations of Central Europe—Poland, Czechoslovakia, Hungary, Roumania, Bulgaria, and Yugoslavia—have known what it is like to be in the middle of an East-West tug-of-war.

Parentheses serve much the same function, though they are usually more appropriate when you want to suggest that you are inserting a kind of *sotto voce* aside:

The brain (if our theories are correct) is really two brains operating simultaneously.

or explanatory information:

Lamarck (1744–1829) was a French naturalist and pre-Darwinian evolutionist.

The poetry of the *fin de siècle* (end of the century) period was characterized by a world-weariness and fashionable despair that was closer to intellectual vapidity than spiritual emptiness.

Series

The least complicated punctuation is that of the series. Once a teacher or supervisor decides for you whether or not you use a comma before the *and,* you don't have too many more decisions:

His wit, his *charm, and his* appearance made him everyone's friend.

His wit, his *charm and* his appearance made him everyone's favorite.

Whichever you choose, be consistent. The advantage in always putting the comma before *and* is that you'll never confuse a reader about whether the last two items are supposed to be taken as a unit or separately:

> The Treasurer will issue separate reports on the yields for Treasury notes, grain futures, common *stocks and bonds.*

If any of the items in the series needs internal commas, then use semicolons to set off the items:

> In mystery novels, the principal action ought to be economical, organic, and *logical; fascinating,* yet not *exotic; clear* but complicated enough to hold the reader's interest—a compromise that is not always easy to strike.

How you punctuate a series of adjectives before a noun depends on whether you intend them to be rhetorically equal or increasingly specific:

> Everyone likes a big red juicy apple.

> We shall eliminate all nonfunctioning, nonrepairable, obsolete units.

Big is more general than *red, red* more general than *juicy,* so we put them in that order without commas. Compare: *a juicy red big apple.* But *nonfunctioning, nonrepairable,* and *obsolete* are equally specific, so we coordinate them with commas. Compare: *an obsolete, nonrepairable, nonfunctioning unit,* a phrase just as acceptable as the original.

A FINE POINT

Ordinarily, don't put a comma between a pair of coordinated items:

> As computers become more *sophisticated, and more powerful,* they have taken over more *clerical, and bookkeeping* tasks.

> As computers become more *sophisticated and more powerful,* they have taken over more *clerical and bookkeeping* tasks.

There are, however, some exceptions:

1. If you want a more intense effect, drop out the *and* and insert a comma. Compare:

   Abraham Lincoln never had the advantage of *a formal education and never owned* a large library.

   Abraham Lincoln never had the advantage of *a formal education, never owned* a large library.

   The great lesson of the pioneers was to stop complaining about conditions that seem difficult or *even overwhelming and to get on* with the business of shaping a life in a hostile environment.

   The great lesson of the pioneers was to stop complaining about conditions that seem difficult or *even overwhelming, to get on with* the business of shaping a life in a hostile environment.

2. A long coordinate pair occasionally needs a comma to interrupt what otherwise would be a monotonous flow:

   It is in the graveyard scene that Hamlet finally realizes that the inevitable end of all life is the *grave and that regardless* of one's station in life the end of all pretentiousness and all plotting and counterplotting must be clay.

   It is in the graveyard scene that Hamlet finally realizes that the inevitable end of all life is the *grave, and that regardless* of one's station in life, the end of all pretentiousness and all plotting and counterplotting must be clay.

3. Sometimes, we put a comma even after a short coordinate member if we want a dramatic pause:

   These data are rather *thin, and even inaccurate.*

   The ocean is one of nature's most glorious *creations, and one of its most destructive.*

This is especially common before a *but:*

   Organ transplants are becoming increasingly *common, but* not less expensive.

4. And finally, we can put a comma after a short or long

coordinate member if we might mislead our reader about
the grammar of a sentence:

Conrad's *Heart of Darkness* inquires into those primitive impulses
that lie deep in each of us and stir only in our darkest dreams
and asserts the unassailable need for the civilized values and
institutions that control those impulses.

A comma after *dreams* would clearly mark the end of one coordinate
member and the beginning of the next:

Conrad's *Heart of Darkness* inquires into those primitive impulses
that lie deep in each of us and stir only in our darkest *dreams, and
asserts* the unassailable need for the civilized values and institutions
that control those impulses.

Exercise 10-I

Here are two passages minus all their original punctuation. Extra
spacings   indicate boundaries of grammatical sentences. Punctuate these passages twice, once using the least punctuation possible,
then a second time using as much varied punctuation as you can.
Then do it a third time in the way that you think most effective.

1. From all available evidence no black man had ever set foot
   in this tiny Swiss village before I came   I was told before
   arriving that I would probably be a "sight" for the village
        I took this to mean that people of my complexion were
   rarely seen in Switzerland and also that people are always
   something of a "sight" outside the city   it did not occur to
   me possibly because I am an American that there could be
   people anywhere who had never seen a Negro   it is a fact
   that cannot be explained on the basis of the   inaccessibility of the village   the village is very high   but it is
   only four hours from Milan and three hours from
   Lausanne   it is true that it is virtually unknown   few
   people making plans for a holiday would elect to come
   here   on the other hand the villagers are able presumably
   to come and go as they please which they do to another
   town at the foot of the mountain with a population of
   approximately five thousand the nearest place to see a

movie or go to the bank   in the village there is no movie
house no bank no library no theater very few radios one
jeep one station wagon and at the moment one typewriter
mine an invention which the woman next door to me here
had never seen   there are about six hundred people living
here all Catholic   I conclude this from the fact that the
Catholic church is open all year round whereas the
Protestant chapel set off on a hill a little removed from the
village is open only in the summertime when.the tourists
arrive   there are four or five hotels all closed now and
four or five bistros of which however only two do any
business during the winter   these two do not do a great
deal   for life in the village seems to end around nine or
ten o'clock   there are a few stores butcher baker *épicerie,* a
hardware store and a moneychanger who cannot change
travelers' checks but must send them down to the bank an
operation which takes two or three days   there is
something called the Ballet Hall closed in the winter and
used for God knows what certainly not ballet in the
summer   there seems to be only one schoolhouse in the
village and this for the quite young children

—James Baldwin, "Stranger in the Village," from *Notes of a Native Son*

2. In fact of course the notion of universal knowledge has
   always been an illusion   but it is an illusion fostered by
   the monistic view of the world in which a few great central
   truths determine in all its wonderful and amazing
   proliferation everything else that is true   we are not today
   tempted to search for these keys that unlock the whole of
   human knowledge and of man's experience   we know that
   we are ignorant   we are well taught it   and the more
   surely and deeply we know our own job the better able we
   are to appreciate the full measure of our pervasive
   ignorance   we know that these are inherent limits
   compounded no doubt and exaggerated by that sloth and
   that complacency without which we would not be men at
   all   but knowledge rests on knowlege   what is new is
   meaningful because it departs slightly from what was
   known before   this is a world of frontiers where even the

liveliest of actors or observers will be absent most of the time from most of them   perhaps this sense was not so sharp in the village that village which we have learned a little about but probably do not understand too well the village of slow change and isolation and fixed culture which evokes our nostalgia even if not our full comprehension   perhaps in the villages men were not so lonely   perhaps they found in each other a fixed community a fixed and only slowly growing store of knowledge of a single world   even that we may doubt   for there seem to be always in the culture of such times and places vast domains of mystery if not unknowable then imperfectly known endless and open

> —J. Robert Oppenheimer, "The Sciences and Man's Community," from *Science and the Common Understanding*

SUMMING UP: REASONABLE PUNCTUATION

1. At the end of a grammatical sentence, use one of the following.
   a. A period, question mark, or exclamation point, even if the next sentence begins with *and, but, yet, for, so, or, nor:*
   At first, the group was strangely *unresponsive. But* as the meeting progressed, they became more animated.
   b. A semicolon if the next grammatical sentence does not begin with *and, but, yet, for, so, or, nor:*
   Imagination is not a literary *gift; it* is part of being a human being.
   c. A comma, if the next grammatical sentence begins with *and, but, yet, for, so, or, nor:*
   It is true, as Marshall McLuhan says, that the medium is the message, but it is also true that the message is considerably more than just the medium.

But if the first grammatical sentence has a good deal of internal punctuation, don't hesitate to use a semicolon before the conjunction:

In the sciences, new facts, new theories, are not merely added to the sum of knowledge, regardless of how long and how established that sum of knowledge *might be; nor do* those new facts and new theories merely replace the old, as a new brick completely fills the space of one that has been removed and discarded.

d. A colon, if what follows the colon is a list, a restatement, a consequence, conclusion, illustration, etc., of the first sentence:

Harry Truman entered office as one of the least promising of our *presidents: He had been* a minor senator from Missouri, an obedient political partyman, and someone who Roosevelt believed would best serve his country by presiding over the Senate, quietly.

e. Just a comma, if the grammatical sentences are short, do not contain internal punctuation, and are closely related and rhetorically balanced:

I *came, I saw, I* went away impressed.

f. Just an *and, but, yet, so, for, or, nor,* if both grammatical sentences are short and balanced:

American fishermen argued for a 200-mile *limit and the American public* supported them.

Many tried to turn Einstein into a political *pundit but he* would have none of it.

Compare:

Texas and Louisiana have requested that Mexico pay for the recent oil spill that polluted their coasts and damaged their fishing and tourist *industry, but Mexico* has flatly refused.

No public official has the right to set him- or herself above the *law, and it's* clear that the American public is not about to change that principle.

g. A dash if the following grammatical sentence is short and dramatic:

We are all a product of our *environment—so why* do we abuse it?

2. At the beginning of a grammatical sentence, use the following punctuation:

   a. Nothing after conjunctions such as *because, if, when, after, although, unless, before, since, as.* Not:

   Academic freedom is the foundation of a free society *because, it* prevents the state from using the educational system for its own ends.

   b. Nothing after *and, but, yet, for, so, nor, or.* Not:

   Both Kennedy and Nixon were qualified to be President in 1960. *But, Kennedy* knew how to manipulate the media more effectively.

   c. A comma after a word or phrase that relates to the whole of the following sentence:

   Therefore, to appreciate ballet is to appreciate both animal grace and the grace of intellect.

   d. A comma if your reader can mistake the grammar of a sentence. Not:

   If you want to *improve [,] your mind* and your soul must be disciplined.

   e. A comma after a long (more than six or so words) introductory element:

   Regardless of any appearance of random or even accidental form, a work of modern art always implies a deliberate intention.

   f. A dash or a colon between a subject consisting of a list and a word that summarizes the list:

   Copernicus, Galileo, Newton, Darwin, Freud, Einstein—they did not give us new and unfamiliar things to look at so much as new ways to look at familiar things.

   The freedom to travel, to worship, to read what we will, to gather and discuss the conduct of our lives: Such privileges are unknown in most of the world.

3. Inside a sentence, punctuate as follows:

   a. Set off obvious interruptions with commas or dashes:

The woman's *movement—I use the term loosely and inclusively—has* brought together many women who otherwise never would have met.

A *nation, they say, gets* the government it deserves.

b. Set off parenthetical, nonrestrictive, loosely added material with commas, with parentheses (infrequently), or with dashes (even more infrequently):

Toscanini, who assuredly will be remembered as the premier maestro of the twentieth century, never exaggerated his own abilities.

During this period *(from roughly the middle of June to the end of summer),* Allied forces advanced very slowly.

Every *ruler—king, president, prime minister, or tyrant—surrounds* himself with advisers who will assure him he is always right.

c. Set off items in a list with a comma, or if those items are themselves punctuated with commas, with a semicolon:

This will require *money, effort, and* time.

I shall first discuss Hamlet, a tragedy of the *intellect; then Lear,* a tragedy of the *heart; and* finally *Macbeth,* a tragedy of the soul.

4. Separate two coordinated items with a comma under the following conditions.

a. When the beginning of the second element can be mistaken:

We must continue to believe that we can shape our future and achieve our *goal, and resolutely* dedicate ourselves to that effort.

b. When the first item is so long that its rhythm becomes monotonous:

Myths constitute the record of those prehistorical events that have given shape to a preliterate *culture, and give dramatic power* to the cultural values that hold that shape.

c. When you want to give the second member a dramatic turn:

We must never underestimate the power of an aroused *citizenry, or overestimate* it.

Appendix

Some Terms Defined

There is a satisfactory boniness about grammar which the flesh of sheer vocabulary requires before it can become vertebrate and walk the earth. But to study it for its own sake, without relating it to function, is utter madness.

Anthony Burgess

Thou hast most traitorously corrupted the youth of the realm in erecting a grammar school. . . . It will be proved to thy face that thou hast men about thee that usually talk of a noun and a verb, and such abominable words as no Christian ear can endure to hear.

William Shakespeare, 2 Henry VI, 4.7

What follows is not a tightly systematic glossary of grammatical terminology. It is rather some generally reliable advice about how to understand the terms starred in the text, *for the purposes of this text,* and how to identify examples of what they refer to. Each definition has its exceptions, but each remains serviceable for the study of style.

Action: For our purposes here, a very broad concept. It includes all movement, feeling, cogitation, creation, attention, condition, etc. Typically, an action is expressed by a verb*: *move, hate, think, discover, watch.* But it may be expressed as a noun*: *movement, hatred, thought, discovery.* Conditions are typically expressed by adjectives*: *careful, intelligent, large, transparent;* but these, too, may be expressed by nouns: *carefulness, intelligence, largeness, transparency.* Some actions may be expressed only by nouns: *motion, transition, contempt.*

Active: An active verb* usually (not always) has the doer of its action* as its subject* and never occurs in its past participle* form after a form of *be.* It may occur in its past participle form after *have:*

I have *checked* the results.

or it may occur after *be* if the verb is in its present participle* form:

I am *checking* the results.

A passive* verb always has as its subject* that toward which an action is directed. It always occurs in its past participle form after a form of *be* (or *get*):

The results have *been checked.*

The results are *being checked.*

Adjective: An adjective describes a noun. You can identify adjectives by putting a *very* in front of a word you think might be one: *very old, very intelligent, very interesting, very fascinated.* There are a few words we might want to call adjectives that this test will not identify: *major, additional, resumptive, occupational,* etc. You can identify such words as adjectives by trying them out between *the* and an appropriate noun: *The **occupational** hazard, the **major** reason, an **additional** problem,* etc. Unfortunately, because some nouns occur in the same place: *the **garden** path, the **stone** wall,* this method is not always reliable.

Adjective Phrase: An adjective* and whatever attaches to it:

> *so*   *large*   ***that no one could carry it***

Adverb: This term refers to a potpourri of items. Adverbs are words that modify parts of speech other than nouns*. Adverbs can modify

> Adjectives*: ***extremely** large, **rather** old, **very** tired*
>
> Verbs*:   ***frequently** spoke, **often** slept, left **here***
>
> Adverbs: *very carefully, **somewhat** often, **a bit** late*
>
> Articles*:   ***precisely** the man I meant, **just** the thing we need*
>
> Whole sentences*:   ***Fortunately,** we were on time; **consequently,** we saw the show.*

Adverb Phrase: The adverb* and whatever attaches to it:

> *too*   ***carefully***   *to be accidental*

Agent: The originating force of an action*, the source of an action, the responsible party, that entity without which an action could not occur.

Article: *a, the, this, that, these, those.*

Clause: Except for imperatives *(Come here!),* a clause has a subject* and a verb* that can be in a past or present form (it's called a finite* verb: *goes, went;* as opposed to an infinitive* verb: *to go).* These are all clauses:

> He left.
>
> Because he left

Why   he left

That   he left

By this definition, *for him to leave* is not a clause, because the verb *leave* is in its infinitive form, not in its finite form; nor is *his examining the document* a clause, because the verb is in its present participle* form.

There are two kinds of clauses: *subordinate,* and *main* (or independent). Subordinate clauses usually begin with some kind of subordinating conjunction*.

Adverbial subordinate clauses comment on time, cause, condition, etc. They usually begin with words such as *because, although, when, if, since, before, as, after, while, unless:*

Unless *you leave,* I will take action.

Because *you have not left,* I've called the police.

When *you leave,* close the door.

Adjectival* subordinate clauses describe nouns*. They are also called relative* clauses and usually begin with the relative pronouns *which, that, whom, whose, who:*

The book **that** *I bought for you* is expensive.

My car, **which** *you just saw,* is gone.

A woman **whose** *aunt lives down the street* just called.

Subordinate clauses that function like nouns usually begin with *that, what, why, how, who, when, where, whether:*

I don't know **what** *I should do.*

That *she is not here* worries me.

I'll ask **whether** *we can stay.*

I already told you **who** *came.*

There are exceptions in all three cases. In this next sentence, the three subordinate clauses are introduced by an adverbial *if,* a relative *which,* and a subordinating conjunction, *that:*

If we had the resources *which* you have described, I don't doubt *that* we could do better.

But we can omit them:

[   ] Had we the resources [   ] you have described, I don't doubt [   ] we could do better.

Main, or independent, clauses have their own subject and finite verb and do not function as an adjective, adverb, or noun.

Complement: A complement completes a verb* that needs completing, that is unfinished without something following it (including direct objects*):

I   am   *in the house.*

We   seem   *tired.*

She   discovered   *the money.*

He   began   *to do the job.*

Compound Noun: You can't tell from spelling alone when a pair of words is a compound noun. Some are separate words: *space capsule, retirement home, police station;* some are hyphenated: *mother-in-law, eighty-two;* some are written as one word: *fireman, airport, bookkeeper.* A reliable test is pronunciation: If the first word is stressed more than the second, the word is a compound word: *dóg hoùse, spáce càpsule, bóok deàler.* On the other hand, some phrases that seem to be compounds are stressed on the second word: *gàrden páth, stòne wáll, fàther cónfessor.*

Conjunction: Usually defined as a word that links two other words, phrases*, or clauses*, but verbs* and prepositions* do the same thing. It's easier to illustrate conjunctions than to define them precisely.

Adverbial conjunctions: *because, although, when, since, if, unless, while, after,* etc.

(See *adverbial clause* under Clause*.)

Relative conjunction or relative pronoun: *who, whom, whose, which, that*

(See *relative clause* under Clause*.)

Sentence conjunction: *thus, however, therefore, consequently, nevertheless, on the other hand, in fact,* etc.

Coordinating conjunction: *and, but, yet, for, so, or, nor*

(See Coordination*.)

Correlative coordinating* conjunctions: *both X and Y, not only X but Y, either X or Y, neither X nor Y, X as well as Y*

Coordination: We coordinate grammatically equal elements:

Words: *you **and** me, red **and** black, run **or** jump, old **yet** strong*

Phrases: *in the house **but** not in the basement, very young **and** very smart*

Clauses*: *when I leave **or** when you arrive*

Ordinarily, the phrases and clauses have to be of the same grammatical order:

Not: *for him to leave **and** that she stayed*

But: *that he left **and** that she stayed*

Or: *for him to leave **and** for her to stay*

Correlative Conjunction: See Conjunction.* Ordinarily, the second member of the correlative conjunction pair should come just before a phrase or clause that is identical to the phrase or clause that precedes it:

Not: He **both** *had the data **and** the equipment* to display it.

But: He had **both** *the data **and** the equipment* to display it.

Not: The shipment will **either** *arrive on Monday **or** on Wednesday.*

But: The shipment will arrive **either** *on Monday **or** on Wednesday.*

Or: The shipment will arrive on **either** *Monday **or** Wednesday.*

Finite Verb: See Verb*.

Free Modifier: A phrase added to the end of a clause that modifies the subject of the clause:

> She walked down the street, *ready for anything.*
>
> I tried to explain the problem, *pointing out all the difficulties.*
>
> The fire engine appeared, *siren screaming.*

Goal: That toward which an action* seems to be directed. It may be that which is affected, created, observed, perceived, changed, etc. In most cases, goals are expressed as direct objects*: In some cases, the goal can be the subject* of an active* sentence*:

> *I* underwent an interrogation.   I see *you.*
>
> *She* received a warm welcome.   I broke *the dish.*
>
>   I built *a house.*

Grammatical Sentence: A sentence that cannot be separated by a period into two sentences that could stand by themselves. Traditional grammarians call these *simple* and *complex* sentences:

> Simple: *The bureau* in London *is* no longer responsible for overseas planning, making it a less influential office.
>
> Complex: *The bureau* in London *is* no longer responsible for overseas planning, [because *we have* centralized operations].

Neither of these can be broken into two sentences with a period. When a single punctuated sentence contains more than one grammatical sentence, traditional grammarians call it a *compound sentence* if each of the grammatical sentences has only one main clause*:

> Cleveland won, and Washington lost.

If the punctuated sentence contains two main clauses and a

subordinate clause* attached to either or to both, then traditional grammarians call it a *compound-complex* sentence:

> We stayed because we had paid in advance, but they left.

We can change the first to two simple sentences and the second to a complex and a simple sentence merely by separating them with periods before *and* and *but*.

The difference between traditional terminology and the terminology I have used here is important: When we talk about "long" sentences, we may have to distinguish a long punctuated sentence from a long grammatical sentence. When a long punctuated sentence is made up of several grammatical sentences (compound or compound-complex in the terminology of traditional grammar), a reader can usually follow it much more easily than he can a long punctuated sentence made up of a single grammatical sentence.

Independent Clause: See Clause*.

Infinitive: See Verb*.

Inflection: See Verb*.

Intransitive Verb: A kind of verb* that does not take an object* and cannot be made into a passive* verb. These are not transitive* verbs:

> He *exists*. They *left* town. She *became* a queen.

Linking Verb: A verb whose complement* modifies or refers to the same thing as its subject*. Linking verbs are a kind of intransitive* verb.

> Linking: He *is* my brother. She *seems* reliable. They *became* teachers. It *appears* broken.

Main Clause: See Clause*.

Metadiscourse: Writing about writing, whatever does not refer to the subject matter being addressed. This includes all connecting devices such as *therefore, however, for example, in the first place;* all comment about the author's attitude: *I believe, in my opinion, let me also point out;* all comment about the writer's confidence in his following assertion: *most people believe, it is widely assumed, allegedly;* references to the audience: *as you can see, you will find that, consider now the problem of.* . . .

Nominalization: A noun* based on, derived from, communicating the same information as a verb* or adjective*: *move–movement, act–action, resist–resistance, good–goodness, intelligent–intelligence, elastic–elasticity.*

Nonrestrictive Clause: See Clause*.

Noun: A word that will fit into the following position: The _____ is good.

Object: There are three kinds of objects: (1) prepositional object: the noun* that follows a preposition* *(in **the house,** by **the walk,** across **the street,** with **fervor**)*; (2) direct object: the noun that follows a transitive verb* *(I read **the book,** we followed **the car**)*; (3) indirect object: a noun or pronoun directly after a verb, preceding a direct object. The same noun or pronoun can also appear as the object of a preposition following a direct object:

I gave *my friend* a book.

I gave   a book *to my friend.*

He bought *me* some flowers.

He bought   some flowers for me.

Orienter: A word or phrase, usually occurring at the beginning of a sentence* or clause*, that sets what follows in a time or place, or gives the reader a point of view toward what follows, or provides some other context that allows a reader to understand an assertion correctly:

In the morning, insects are relatively inactive.

Politically speaking, the Old Left has little influence anymore.

Under most circumstances, mammals will fight to protect their young.

Passive: See Active*.

Past Participle: Most verbs signal past participle forms with *-ed: walked, jumped, worked, investigated.* Irregular verbs have irregular past participle forms: *seen, broken, swum, stolen, hurt, been,* etc. When they follow a *have,* they are in their "perfect" form:

I *have* **gone**. Her friends *have* **arrived**. We *had* **been** there.

Past participle forms also function as modifiers:

a *broken* arm, a *twisted* leg, a *scratched* face.

Phrase: A group of words that constitute a unit but do not include a subject* and a finite verb*. There are noun phrases, which center on a noun* and may include modifying elements: *the little **book** on the table*; verb phrases: *may have been **found***; and adjective* and adverb* phrases.

Predicate: Whatever follows the subject*: *He **went downtown yesterday to buy a suit**.* Whatever introduces a sentence that could appear with the predicate is also part of the predicate: **Yesterday,** he **went downtown**.

Preposition: Like conjunctions,* prepositions are easier to list than to define: *in, on, up, over, out, under, between, at, toward, with, by, across,* etc.

Prepositional Phrase: The preposition* plus its *noun* object*: in the house, by the door, without enthusiasm.*

Present Participle: The *-ing* form of the verb. It can be used as the *progressive* form of the verb (always following a form of *be*):

He was *running*. I am *listening*. You *are going*.

or as the *gerundive* form, the form that functions as a noun:

Running is good for you. *Listening* is important.

or as a modifier:

Running streams are beautiful. *Working* wives are common.

Progressive: See Verb*.

Punctuated Sentence: Whatever begins with a capital letter and ends with a period, question mark, or exclamation point.

Relative Clause: See Clause*.

Relative Pronoun: See Clause*.

Restrictive Clause: See Clause*.

Resumptive Modifier: A resumptive modifier is added to the end of a phrase or clause. It repeats a word used at or near the end of that phrase or clause.

> East Coast columnists and commentators delight in expressing their own narrow *view* of the world,
> *a view* . . .

To this repeated word is added more information:

> . . . own narrow *view* of the world, *a view* shaped by the insular and heated intellectualism that characterizes the East Coast liberal establishment.

Sentence: There is no easy definition for *sentence* that would be useful here. It's useful to distinguish two kinds, however: grammatical sentence* and punctuated sentence*.

Stress: The end of the sentence*, what should be the location of your most important ideas.

Subject: The subject is whatever the verb* agrees with in person and number:

> *Two men* ***are*** at the door.

> *One man* ***is*** at the door.

We can see that *there* in

> There ***was*** *a man* at the door.

> There ***were*** *two men* at the door.

is the subject of neither sentence. It is merely a function word that fills the slot that we expect before a verb.

You can always identify a subject once you have identified the verb: Simply put a *who* or a *what* in front of the verb and turn the sentence into a question. The answer to the question is the subject of the sentence:

> That ontogeny recapitulates phylogeny *is* an accepted evolutionary fact.

> Question: ***What*** *is* an accepted evolutionary fact?

> Answer (and subject): That ontogeny recapitulates phylogeny.

> (This doesn't work with sentences beginning with *there*.)

Subordinate Clause: See Clause*.

Subordinating Conjunction: *Because, if, when, since, although*

Summative Modifier: A summative modifier occurs at the end of a clause. It begins by summing up the clause:

> Some economists believe the price of gold will go to $1,000 an ounce,
> > *an opinion . . .*

It then continues with a modifying phrase or clause:

> . . . to $1,000 an ounce,
>> *an opinion* that is not shared by all of
>> them.

Topic: The idea that a sentence* comments on. It is what the sentence is about. It is usually the subject* of a sentence:

> *China* will eventually become a major industrial nation.

But the topic can appear in other places:

> In regard to *China,* it will eventually become. . . .
>
> I believe that *China* will eventually become. . . .
>
> There is general agreement as to *China's* eventually becoming a major industrial nation.

Transitive Verb: A verb* with a direct object*. The object can be made the subject* of a passive* verb:

> We *read* the book.
> The book *was read* by us.

By this definition, the verbs *resemble, become, stand* (as in *He stands ten feet tall*) are not transitive verbs.

Verb: Verbs have four forms:
Infinitive: The "bare," or base, form of the verb: *go, be, have.* In many cases, the infinitive form follows a *to: He wants to **leave.***
Finite: The verb inflected for present or past: *went, was, were, has, does, sees.* There is no difference between the infinitive and finite forms when the finite form refers to the present and does not have a third-person *s:*

> I *see* the book.
>
> I want to *see* the book.

You can always identify the main verb in a clause* because it is also the finite form of the verb. To find out which word that is, just change the time the clause refers to. If the clause refers to the past, change it to refer to the present; if to the present, change it to the past; if to the future, to either past or present. The word you have to change is the finite verb:

He *decided* to leave.   He *decides* to leave.
He *left*.   He *leaves*.

Answers to Exercises

Few of these exercises have a single correct answer: A good many of your answers will be different from but as good as those here; indeed, I would be surprised if many were not better. Trust your ear. If you decide your version is better than the answer here, try to state why: Don't depend on generalities like clarity and precision. Try to say *why* it's clearer and more precise: Is it shorter? Is it more specific? If your answers are less compact and direct than those suggested here, try to decide whether the difference between your version and mine is a significant difference. There comes a point in every sentence where another five minutes spent looking for the most concise and specific version possible is simply not worth the result. It's the first five minutes that count.

Exercise 2-I

1. We expected to establish new tolerance levels.
2. The engineering staff attempted to assess the project.
3. The governing committee announced that they would submit their report by the deadline.
4. The candidate appeared before the board on June 30th.
5. The governor must refuse the request.
6. The President appealed to the American people to conserve gasoline.
7. At that time, independent investigators measured the half-life of thorium more accurately.
8. The participants discussed the future of the program amicably.
9. The business sector did not independently analyze what caused the trade deficit. (did not attempt to analyze why trade was in the red)
10. The two sides agreed that they had to revise the terms of the treaty.
11. Management was uneasy over the result of the survey.
12. The laboratory personnel must thoroughly prepare the specimen sections.

13. The insurer must check the discrepancy in the data.
14. We did not expect the dean to reject the application.
15. The police immediately investigated the affair.
16. Do not hesitate to say no.
17. After the last report, we studied the same principles of bilateral symmetry.
18. The Air Force will never solve the problem of UFOs.
19. I believe that the administrators should consult with the student body before anyone changes the rules.
20. We must cut back on loans because we failed to acquire federal funding.
21. They must redetermine what personnel they need before local sources can assist them.
22. The surgeon may replace corneal tissue completely only if immunoresponse mechanisms have been suppressed (if he can suppress . . .).
23. I would oversimplify the problem if I argued that all government officials administered their programs inefficiently.
24. Goywzc contributed to the literature significantly when he specified why people emigrate from environments that lack a sufficient capital base (G. made a significant contribution to . . .).
25. Although social scientists have been developing ways to corroborate that their respondents have responded reliably and validly, Jones did not employ any of them in this study; as a result, we cannot rely on his respondents' exaggerated estimates of their situations.
26. Let me give you the most important reason why you should try to write as clearly and as directly as you can: When you grind out a sentence choked with abstract nouns and limp passives, a sentence that seems more like a syntactic labyrinth than an attempt to speak directly to the mind of your audience, you risk deceiving not only that audience but even yourself. When you write a sentence that reverberates with the rumbling of one Latinate noun after another, you may believe that you have said something important, regardless of what you have actually said. When you edit that rumble away, you may find that what you thought was thundering prose is in reality the echo of an empty barrel.

Exercise 2-II

1. The committee on standards for plant safety discussed recent announcements of regulations regarding air quality.
2. We can reduce blood pressure in diabetic patients if we apply depressor agents from renal extract.

3. Phenomena involving the pancreatic gland are regulated chiefly by cells in the parasympathetic nervous system.
4. The main goal of this article is to describe how readers comprehend texts and produce protocols for recall.
5. On the basis of these principles, we may now attempt to formulate rules by which we extract information from narratives.
6. This paper investigates how information is processed in games where computers simulate human cognition.
7. The Federal Trade Commission is responsible for enforcing federal guidelines in regard to the durability of tires on new cars.
8. When the defendant appears in court, the presiding justice will effect legal service in the courtroom by requesting that the time requirement be waived so that he can begin to hear the case.
9. The Social Security program guarantees a standard floor for monthly income for individuals whose package of potential benefits is determined by what those individuals have contributed over the course of their lives.
10. After we extensively reviewed the assessments of training needs and visited selected CETA office sites, we identified the concepts and issues that would constitute an initial questionnaire for the staff.
11. Because state law supervises the organization of corporations (how corporations are organized), the federal government is unable to effectively implement measures that would reduce pollution.
12. We could not determine whether the community organizations could be appropriately supported because it was difficult for us to obtain relevant data when we reviewed the activities of the committees.
13. On November 1, 1979, the secretary of the Department of Energy announced in a press release that after the Department of Energy and major manufacturers met on October 28 to discuss the matter, the manufacturers decided to dispose of their surplus stock of alcohol.
14. These reimbursements have been improperly claimed because relevant school personnel have failed to comply with policies about reimbursement for food services and because claims for reimbursement have been ineffectively or inadequately reviewed (because X has ineffectively reviewed claims for . . .).
15. In order to interpret cardiac sounds, one must know intimately cardiac physiology and the pathophysiology of cardiac disease.

Exercise 2-III

1. Depending on the rhetorical situation and the interests of the readers, the agents of *reanalyze* and *announce* might or might not be important.
2. Appropriately passive, I think.
3. Trotsky abandons his usual impassioned narrative style and puts in its place a cautious and scholarly treatment of theories of conspiracy (and instead, treats theories of conspiracy in a cautious and scholarly way). But the moment he picks up his narrative line again, he invests his prose. . . .
4. Whether the writer should specify *who* advanced arguments against Darwin depends, I think, on the overall problem the writer is exploring.
5. Almost certainly, we would want to know who has been ignoring the wiretapping regulation: For many years federal, state, and local law enforcement agencies (individuals?) have been regularly ignoring wiretapping restrictions.
6. I believe that I can most clearly explain the social significance of Restoration comedy if I analyze how the plays portray social relationships. In particular, I will study how different social levels interact.
7. We have written these technical directives as simply as possible because we are attempting to communicate more effectively with relatively uneducated employees whom we have hired in accordance with guidelines imposed on us by the federal government.
8. We informed the participants that the county offices would reimburse them, but the state office has decided that the county offices cannot do that at this time.
9. The researchers evaluated tissue rejection according to procedures that most other researchers have abandoned because those procedures consistently overestimated values for the production of antibodies (because those procedures consistently led them to overestimate values for . . .).
10. The ability of the human brain to solve human problems has been universally undervalued because we have not done the research that scientists would consider reliable.

Exercise 3-I

1. The agencies that assist participants in our programs have reversed their recently announced policy to return to their original one.
2. Critics must use abstract terms to analyze and discuss literary texts.

3. Science depends on accurate data if it is to offer ideas that will allow mankind to advance safely.
4. Even though education is important to the development of our children, some groups and individuals object to fair taxes that provide a decent education.
5. Most patients at public clinics probably accept general medical treatment because their problems are rather minor and can be treated with understanding and attention.

Exercise 3-II

1. Graduate students looking for good teaching jobs face an uncertain future.
2. Even though gun laws are being heatedly debated, the public must continue to discuss them.
3. When investors believe that inflation will continue to grow, they usually invest in works of art.
4. If state governors could discuss their respective energy problems, they might find a way to allocate gasoline supplies.
5. Our Founding Fathers never anticipated how lobbyists would influence Congress because they could not predict how powerful business would grow.
6. The most important problem is how much the characters disguise the social tensions in the playwright's society.
7. Teachers have long been interested in how we memorize what we read. The first problem is to identify what features texts do and do not share; the second is to evaluate (measure?) what a person remembers from a text.

Exercise 3-III

1. But TV programming will probably continue to appeal to our most prurient interests.
2. Seborrhea is the abnormal buildup of sebacious matter, forming scabs or encrustations.
3. The person we call Shakespeare could be someone else, perhaps even royalty.
4. We need to approach plea bargaining in a new way for two reasons. First, plea bargaining lets hardened criminals escape their just punishment; and second, it encourages a lack of respect for the judicial system.

5. Finally, China is on the verge of a major industrial expansion.
6. Next, three principles can help us decide which wilderness areas to preserve.
7. I do not believe that unexplored parts of the world have snakes larger than those we already know about.
8. Since Trotsky favored the Russian Revolution, he could not be objective about it.
9. Imagism mimics the haiku's strong visual patterns to provoke feeling while it simultaneously rejects the idea that particular feelings correspond to particular images.
10. As for life stages and our mental health, most researchers believe that the midlife crisis is probably the most critical period in our development. It is then that we decide whether we are going to be winners or losers in the game of life.

Exercise 3-IV

1. Inflation will continue if the federal government keeps on spending.
2. We must direct more research to the problems of those who cannot see in low levels of light.
3. Scientists disagree whether the universe is open or closed, a dispute they will resolve only when they have computed the total mass of the universe with an error of no more than 5 percent.
4. So long as taxpayers keep on paying their taxes, the government will be able to pay its debts.
5. We must develop tar sand, oil shale, and coal as sources of fuel, because we must make ourselves invulnerable to foreign powers that at any moment might cut off our oil.
6. We must eliminate carcinogens in meat.
7. We can treat cancer effectively only if we remove the tumor before it metastasizes.
8. Only when Catholics and Protestants resolve the issue of papal authority will they begin to reconcile.
9. When elections deal with those issues that normally escape attention, they will serve their intended function.
10. The Insured must provide the Insurer with all relevant receipts, checks, and other evidence of costs when such expenses exceed $110.
11. Stop taking the medicine only if you are still dizzy and nauseated six hours after you started taking it.

12. Since all the evidence confirms our results, we should accept them, unless we want to consider the fact that other investigations have failed to provide confirming data.
13. You will be prohibited from participating in the cost-sharing education programs only after you have had a hearing into why you were rejected.
14. Since all the HEW-supported public agencies followed the guidelines, their application seems to have been rejected for political reasons.

Exercise 3-V

1. When we look at advertising systematically, we logically begin by defining the term. This establishes a shared point of reference that lets us approach the topic objectively. Unfortunately, because we must define advertising in so many ways, it makes it likely that we will be subjective. That indicates that we must examine popular notions about advertising carefully.
2. Even though we do not know for certain whether life exists elsewhere in the universe, irrefutable statistical evidence argues that life could exist on planetary systems around tens of thousands of stars scattered through the heavens.

Exercise 4-I

1. Responding to the problems we identified in our self-study, this college has already created many activities that meet the expanding needs and interests of our students. These new programs also reflect the traditional goals of the college: the liberal education of the whole person.
2. In their discussion, they juxtaposed two themes: First, because graduate medical training is an apprenticeship, it is basically informal. But, second, in order to train medical students to become competent in their professional knowledge and techniques, graduate medical training must also include some formal instruction in classrooms.
3. It is true that because responsibility is unclearly defined in this organization, its training program has a long history of financial problems and disputes among management. But it is equally true that in the last few years it has placed approximately half of its trainees in jobs equal to their abilities.
4. Being alone and being lonely are different: Which we feel depends on how well we can draw on those resources we developed as we

became adult, that point when we all have to face up to who we are and whether we can live with ourselves.

5. The soaring cost of energy has especially burdened those who can least afford it—the sick, the elderly, those on fixed incomes—all those who can least endure the hardship of lower temperatures. Consequently, we must create a program that would identify such people and then subsidize their fuel costs.

6. Many city dwellers give up on life in the city because the dirt and crime finally defeat them. But when they leave for the country, they often find that they miss the intensity and excitement that makes life in the city so stimulating.

7. Nothing more severely challenges our belief in free speech than the Nazi party of America when it conducts marches and rallies in Jewish communities. These American Nazis want only to enrage those who suffered most from German naziism in order to create a violence that will publicize their party and thereby attract more members and more money.

8. An institution disappearing from our business life is the men-only club that traditionally provided a place to conclude deals in an intimately masculine atmosphere. This is happening because more women are ready to exercise a power that once belonged only to men and are demanding the same amenities that once were the privilege of men alone.

9. In this procedure, we assume the following: (1) We have a sample large enough to include the variation found in the total population; (2) we analyze the data according to accepted statistical procedures; (3) we can replicate the study under conditions the same as those of similar studies.

10. Lear not only fails to recognize that Goneril and Regan are faithless, and that Cordelia and the Fool are honest, but also fails to recognize the disguised Kent. Through flattery like that of Lear's faithless daughters, Kent makes Lear believe that he "serv'sts" him. Even though Kent's intentions are honorable, his flattery is deceitful and exploits and encourages Lear's unreasonable vanity.

Exercise 5-I.
The answers are only exemplary, of course.

1. Many school systems are returning to the basics, basics that have been too long ignored. . . a change that will be welcomed by parents everywhere . . . reasserting the old values that have been ignored for too long.

2. Within the next few years, automobile manufacturers must meet more stringent mileage requirements, requirements that will tax engineering staffs to the utmost . . . a challenge that could tax engineering staffs to the utmost . . . achieving at least a 25 percent increase in efficiency.

3. Why we age is a matter that has puzzled humanity for millennia, a matter that is just now being unraveled . . . a mystery that is just now being unraveled . . . inspiring questions that go to the heart of the human condition.

4. Most young people today cannot even begin to understand the insecurity that people experienced during the Great Depression, an insecurity that still afflicts many who experienced it even today . . . a failure that often makes it difficult or impossible for those different generations to understand one another.

5. The recent fertilization of an embryo in a test tube has raised ethical issues that are troubling both scientists and laypeople, issues that go to the very center of how we define life and humanity . . . an event that will influence both religious and scientific thinking.

6. Many Victorians were appalled when Darwin suggested that their ancestry may have included apes, a response that reflected both political and religious attitudes.

7. In 1961, the U.S. government announced that it would put the first man on the moon, a decision that proved to be one of the best we ever made.

8. Nikita Khrushchev once claimed that by 1975 communism would bury capitalism, a prediction not even he believed at the time.

9. In the 1960s, the Supreme Court ruled that anyone arrested for a crime had to be given the widest benefit of legal doubt, a view not shared by law enforcement officers who had to deal with crime more directly.

10. American prisons are for the most part schools for crime and pits of degradation, a condition that shames a society that claims to be civilized and enlightened.

11. Systematic skepticism denies that we can ever know reality so long as it is screened by human perception, perception that changes reality before we can even begin to contemplate it or even to think about it . . . a point of view that denies both the accuracy of our senses and the intelligence of our minds.

12. Science originated when primitive people observed natural regularities, regularities that eventually became the basis for scientific law and statistically based predictions . . . an intellectual advance upon which all modern thought depends.

13. During the Renaissance, affluent and politically stable scientists allowed streams of thought to flow together, streams of thought

that had both political consequences for every government and intellectual consequences for every European culture . . . a development that changed not only the future but the past as well.

14. Recently, we have witnessed many acts of terrorism, acts that originate in the belief that violence can achieve worthy ends and in the despair that whispers it cannot . . . an indication that the forces of civilization are dissolving and the forces of chaos are increasing.

Exercise 5-II

1. Because Congress failed to anticipate the cost of inflation when it originally voted funds for the Interstate Highway System, the system has run into insoluble problems, problems that could spell the end of the most extensive construction project in world history.

2. Regardless of the reason for it, such conduct is almost always prejudicial to good discipline, undermining morale and encouraging disrespect for authority.

3. Because TV game shows appeal to the cupidity in us all, they are just about the most popular daytime TV, a fact that does not bode well for evening TV.

4. Given the low quality of elected officials, the selection of judges on the basis of merit is an idea whose time came long ago, an idea that will be resisted, however, by most political machines.

5. Working with devices that can accelerate particles almost to the speed of light, researchers in high-energy physics are exploring the ultimate nature of matter, providing us with ever more puzzling facts about the basis of physical existence.

6. Unless we reduce the amount of carbon dioxide we emit into the atmosphere by the end of the century, we will change the climate of the world, a change that could have catastrophic consequences.

7. If before the next congressional election the government does not provide all political candidates with campaign funds, only the rich will be able to seek public office in numbers large enough to assure a wide selection of candidates, numbers that will not, however, include a wide range of political views.

8. Even though smoking and disease correlate statistically, the cigaret companies still insist that no one has scientifically proven that smoking causes disease.

9. In the last half century medical science has learned to detect and even anticipate diseases that would formerly have appeared in our midst and devastated whole populations; it can now predict the outbreak of diseases such as influenza a year in advance, allowing us to prepare for their onslaught.

Exercise 5-III

1. They submitted an ecological impact statement identical to that of the previous year, so it will again be difficult for us to evaluate their data, because we still have no information independently verifying what they supplied.
2. When you obtain EKG readings similar to those obtained earlier, you must suspect conditions other than cardiac insufficiency. In such cases, in order to achieve results as effective as those described in the previous chapter, you must closely adhere to procedures outlined there.
3. Because we have reorganized the division for marketing research, information more accurate than that which we have received in the past should allow us to identify populations different from those we have traditionally aimed at. This information will be relatively easy to analyze because we have already accumulated demographic data such as average income, spending patterns, etc., for many different markets. As a result, we may expect an operation more efficient than that which we conducted last year.

Exercise 5-IV

1. The new barbarians display a range of expressiveness to aesthetic experience that usually takes the form of "Wow."
2. I will now sketch in simple outline the solar system as it was ordinarily conceived by pre-Copernican astronomers.
3. With little sense of scholarly bias, historians impose on the past not just their private view of historical relevancy but the implied view of their whole social matrix.
4. If we study honestly and objectively in all their masculine assumptions the psychoanalytic theories that Freud created for his scholarly and therefore largely male audience, we can perhaps understand why psychiatry has so often assigned to a man's mother the major source of his mental disorders.
5. The next point is the isolation of various clotting mechanisms in higher mammals.
6. A more important defining feature of the modern mind is the ability to relate individual bits of data to general principles applicable at all times and everywhere.
7. It is universally acknowledged that when Woodrow Wilson refused to take into his confidence the leadership of the United States Senate, he caused the defeat of the Treaty of Versailles.
8. The legislative branch comprises two historically antagonistic chambers, one made up of a variety of hereditary and appointed

senators whose responsibility in legislative affairs is relatively slight, the other an elective body that carries on the important legislative activities.

9. Last year in England, though, there was discovered a virus that bears no known relation to any other form of protein-based life.

10. Just as pressing, in the opinion of most international monetary experts, is the need in the years to come to monitor more carefully the flow of hard currency across national boundaries.

11. Because we were unfamiliar with the mechanism, we were not able to detect any metal with it.

12. With every expectation of success, we will begin to try to improve communications.

13. Because the students realized that the undergraduate curriculum had to be revised in the next few weeks, they put proposals on the agenda that had been discussed earlier.

14. After they audited the internal operations conducted in the summer of 1978, they audited the record of those foreign affiliates that had not been audited by their local headquarters. Or: In the summer of 1978, they audited the internal operations; then they audited. . . .

Exercise 6-I

1. Along with the aforementioned summary, we present studies that evaluate the reconstruction of upper and lower eyelids.

2. However, our intuition has been almost completely sublimated by the insidious overgrowth of our belief in the supremacy of rationality.

3. Clearly, in some parts of our country, overbuilding of suburban housing has recently led to extensive flooding and economic disaster.

4. College students often complain about the teacher who assigns a term paper and then gives it only a grade.

5. Under these conditions, fuel lines and steam-heating systems in older coaches have also become frozen.

6. It would be possible, though, to rent books for basic courses—such as mathematics, foreign languages, and English—courses whose textbooks are the same from year to year.

7. At about this time an event occurred that would change the course of the war and of world history.

8. A different matter, we believe, is how to dispose effectively and economically of that which is not biodegradable.

9. To start a dialogue, you can most usefully focus on real community issues rather than talk about broad problems.

10. Moreover, writers of papers should adhere to guidelines for the nonsexist use of language set forth by the NCTE and in the MLA Style Sheet.
11. DuPage County, sixteen miles west of the Loop and covering 338 square miles, has the fastest growing population in the region.
12. First, find an attorney who will respond to your needs and who can translate your organizational problems into the most suitable legal form.

Exercise 6-II

1. This kind of stylistic criticism has two modes: analytic and normative. The analytic critic assumes that the best possible text is the one before him, and that his only task is to explain why the text is as it is. On the other hand, the normative critic assumes that the writer could have missed his intention and then explains where the writer failed to match his language to his ideas. Which form of criticism we choose is determined more by the fame or obscurity of an author than by the intrinsic quality of a text.
2. The discovery of America imposed on the population of discontented Europeans a steady Darwinian selection. The fearful and the least discontented stayed put. The most intrepid and the least rooted gladly gave up everything for the chance to come here. As a result, our gene pool has always favored personality traits that lead to adventurous independence.
3. Except in those areas continually covered with ice or scorched by continual heat, the earth is covered with vegetation. Plants grow not only in richly fertilized plains and river valleys but at the edge of perpetual snow in high mountains, not only in and around lakes and swamps but under the ocean and next to it. They survive in the cracks of busy city sidewalks as well as in barren rocks. Vegetation covered the earth before we existed and will cover the earth long after evolution swallows us up.
4. Abstract expressionism can be defined as a concern with gesture and an awareness of the role of empty space, characteristics that describe the work of many artists who reject the unreal "reality" of philosophical realism. One such artist is Albert Cinque, whose "Study #A" is a play of delicate line against white parchment. No less than the ink, the paper itself becomes part of the medium, with its stark existential spaces overwhelming the spidery yet assertive scrolls.
5. In their natural states, animals do not have the power to create and communicate a new message to fit a new experience. What

they are able to communicate is imposed entirely by their genetic code. For example, when bees communicate information about pollen, they are limited to information about distance, direction, and the richness of the source. In all significant respects, animals are able to communicate only the same limited repertoire of messages over and over in the same fixed way.

Exercise 7–I

1. Your car may have something wrong with one of its parts—the support plate that connects the front suspension to the frame. If the plate fails, you may not be able to steer your car, especially if it fails when you are braking hard. Also, we may have to adjust the catch that holds the hood down, because the secondary catch may be out of line. If it is out of line and the main catch is not secured, your hood could fly up. If the hood flies up, you will not be able to see in front of you. If either the support plate fails or your hood flies up, you could have an accident.
2. Tax collection: Section 3101. The person who employs the taxpayer must deduct this tax from the wages of the employee. These wages may come under one of two headings:
    (1) paragraph (7) (B) or (C), or paragraph (10) of section 3121. During any calendar quarter, the employer may deduct from the employee's wages an amount of money equal to the tax, even if the employer paid his employee less than $50 during that time.
    (2) paragraph (8) (B) of section 3121(a). During any calendar year, the employer may deduct from the employee's wages an amount of money equal to the tax, even in the following circumstances:
        (a) he has paid the employee less than $150 during the calendar year, and
        (b) the employee has not performed agricultural labor for the employer on 20 days or more in the calendar year for cash wages computed on an annual basis.
3. (a) By the words "damages because of bodily injury by accident or disease including death at any time resulting therefrom" we mean this: (1) What it costs to care for the injured person and the value of services that the injured or dead person cannot provide because of the injury or death; (2) the cost of damages that arise when an injured person brings suit against someone we insure, because the injured person is (a) employed by the insured person and (b) injured while working for the insured person.

(b) If you are a policy holder, we will start to pay you or the Bank, as irrevocable creditor-beneficiary, under these conditions: You are insured by us, you are completely disabled by sickness or injury, and you cannot do any part of any paying job for more than thirty consecutive days.

We will compute how much we will pay you as follows: Beginning on the thirty-first day you are disabled, we will pay you for every day you are still disabled according to. . . . We will continue to pay you for any one disability for eighteen months. If you recover sufficiently for us to end payments and then you are disabled again by the same cause, we will compute the period we will pay you as follows: If you are disabled from the same cause within six months after you recovered, we will compute the remaining period we will pay you by subtracting the first period of payments from eighteen months. We will then pay you, as long as you are disabled, for the rest of the eighteen months.

Exercise 7-II

1. The Jimmy Carters and the Teddy Kennedys want to spend my money on counting wild turkeys in Texas and building bigger bombs that will never be used.
2. A New Yorker can't walk down Park Avenue without getting hit over the head.
3. Go to the movies tonight and you won't sleep when you get home.
4. Kiss and The Who spend more money on lights and firecrackers than on their music.
5. Because the corner gas station isn't open on Sundays any more, your neighbors may spend August in their backyard.
6. If I read one more book on how to get in touch with myself, my eyes will roll over in my head.
7. The guy who tightens a bolt every ten seconds on the line at Ford is less interested in another twenty-five cents an hour than he is in a job that he can enjoy.
8. Zap Cereal has as many vitamins and minerals as a chocolate bar.

Exercise 8–I

1. Those who keep silent over the loss of small freedoms will eventually find themselves being kept silent by the loss of large ones.

2. While the strong are never afraid to admit their real weaknesses, the weak are always eager to boast of their imagined strengths.
3. We should pay more attention to those politicians who tell us how to risk making what we have better than to those who tell us how to keep whatever we have from getting worse.
4. When parents raise children who do not value the importance of hard work, the adults those children become invariably resent—because they do not understand—those who work hard to preserve that value.
5. Too many teachers mistake neat papers rehashing conventional ideas for careful logic supporting unexpected truths.
6. Only foolish people and foolish nations trade the next generation's security for their own short-term financial advantage.
7. Never mistake a style that is too difficult to penetrate for ideas that are too complex to understand.
8. We will never solve the energy problem until we start substituting fuels that are entirely replenishable for those that we must one day exhaust.
9. This report does not adequately balance the importance of our immediate cash flow against the need to increase the size of our funded reserves.
10. Only the most naive consumer believes that anyone will sell the secret of making a million dollars for the price of a postage stamp.

Exercise 8-II

1. Few tendencies in our government have changed American life more than the unrestricted power of federal agencies.
2. In 1923, representatives of the Allies went to Versailles to seek the dismemberment of Germany's armaments industry and the destruction of her economic potential.
3. The day is past when boards of education can expect taxpayers to automatically go along with the decisions of extravagant administrators.
4. The blueprint for the campaign was drawn up by the least sensitive of the mayor's advisers.
5. If we invest our sweat in these projects, we must not seem to be working out of self-interest.
6. Irreplaceable works of native art are slowly deteriorating in many of our most prestigious museums because their curators do not recognize the extreme fragility of even recent artifacts.
7. Throughout history, science has advanced because dedicated scientists have overcome the hostility of an uninformed public.

Exercise 8-IV

1. The figures in the first quarter report point to some important facts about productivity, especially how hidden costs are forcing us to cut back our research budget. They reveal how much we need even more research into ways to stop the spiralling wages of unskilled labor.
2. To understand the essence of Einstein's Theory of Relativity, you first have to understand that the speed of light is a constant, regardless of where you stand or what your speed is relative to any other point in the universe. This is an intellectual step few of us can take.
3. We should not too devoutly hope that because we are rational we can make empty space part of our vision of the universe and of our place in it. We will fail because our animal nature prevents us from fully accepting the fact that we are mortal in a transient existence.

Exercise 10-I

1. From all available evidence no black man had ever set foot in this tiny Swiss village before I came. I was told before arriving that I would probably be a "sight" for the village; I took this to mean that people of my complexion were rarely seen in Switzerland, and also that city people are always something of a "sight" outside of the city. It did not occur to me—possibly because I am an American—that there could be people anywhere who had never seen a Negro.

   It is a fact that cannot be explained on the basis of the inaccessibility of the village. The village is very high, but it is only four hours from Milan and three hours from Lausanne. It is true that it is virtually unknown. Few people making plans for a holiday would elect to come here. On the other hand, the villagers are able, presumably, to come and go as they please—which they do: to another town at the foot of the mountain, with a population of approximately five thousand, the nearest place to see a movie or go to the bank. In the village there is no movie house, no bank, no library, no theater; very few radios, one jeep, one station wagon; and at the moment, one typewriter, mine, an invention which the woman next door to me here had never seen. There are about six hundred people living here, all Catholic—I conclude this from the fact that the Catholic church is open all year round, whereas the Protestant chapel, set off on a hill a little removed from the village, is open only in the summertime when the tourists arrive. There are four or five hotels, all closed now, and four or five *bistros,* of which, however, only two do any business during the winter. These two do not do a great deal, for life in the village seems to end around nine or ten o'clock. There are a few stores, butcher, baker, *épicerie,* a hardware store, and a money-changer—who cannot change travelers' checks, but must send them down to the bank, an operation which takes two or three days. There is something called the *Ballet Haus,* closed in the winter and used for God knows what, certainly not ballet, during the summer. There seems to be only one schoolhouse in the village, and this for the quite young children.

2. In fact, of course, the notion of universal knowledge has always been an illusion; but it is an illusion fostered by the monistic view of the world in which a few great central truths determine in all its wonderful and amazing proliferation everything else that is true. We are not today tempted to search for these keys that unlock the whole of human knowledge and of man's experience. We know that we are ignorant; we are well taught it, and the more surely and deeply we know our own job the better able we are to appreciate the full measure of our pervasive ignorance. We know that these are inherent limits, compounded, no doubt, and exaggerated by that sloth and that complacency without which we would not be men at all.

   But knowledge rests on knowledge; what is new is meaningful because it departs slightly from what was known before; this is a world of frontiers, where even the liveliest of actors or observers will be absent most of the time from most of them. Perhaps this sense was not so sharp in the village—that village which we have learned a little about but probably do not understand too well—the village of slow change and isolation and fixed culture which evokes our nostalgia even if not our full comprehension. Perhaps in the villages men were not so lonely; perhaps they found in each other a fixed community, a fixed and only slowly growing store of knowledge—a single world. Even that we may doubt, for there seem to be always in the culture of such times and places vast domains of mystery, if not unknowable, then imperfectly known, endless and open.

Index